THE DANGER
WE SURVIVED

THE DANGER
WE SURVIVED

By Augustus T. Porter

Xulon Press

Xulon Press
2301 Lucien Way #415
Maitland, FL 32751
407.339.4217
www.xulonpress.com

© 2018 by Augustus T. Porter

Cover design: Martin Carenzo

What you are about to read is my true story. The events in this book are classified as
historical non-fiction.

Printed in the United States of America.

ISBN-13: 9781545624364

To my beloved brother
Fallah Porter Jr.

The right of every individual to live and prosper must be exercised in every corner of our planet.

— Augustus T. Porter

TABLE OF CONTENTS

ACKNOWLEDGMENTS

MY HEART AND my arms cannot extend enough to reach those who have provided us with unconditional shelter in helpless times.

My unheard voice opens this sound to express my endless gratitude to the unknown heroes that are changing lives in their little corners in ways that they can. The completion of this undertaking could not have been possible without the participation and assistance of so many people whose names may not all be enumerated. Their contributions to my success in life are sincerely appreciated and gratefully acknowledged. However, I would like to express my deep appreciation and indebtedness particularly to the following:

My beloved parents (Mr. & Mrs Fallah & Sarah Porter); My beautiful kids (Demetria, Saah and Sia) and my wonderful Sister and Husband (Rose & Joseph Swaray).

To Gary UMC family, Wheaton IL., World Relief Dupage, the People's Resource Center, the city of Wheaton and College of Dupage for all your support. My faithful friends Rick and Renee Carlson, Bill and Vickie Austin, David and Heidi Brewer,

Teresa and David Exner, Don and Barbara Garlinger, Debra Hafner, Mike Capra, Beverly Holze, Dave Roe, Don and Judy Leo, Dr. Tracy Malone, Rev. Jamie Geiger and Rev. Christopher Pierson. To Dominique Steward, Professor Robert Dixon Kolar, the staff and students of the Global Studies Program (College of Dupage).

In Texas, I am grateful to my friends, Walt and Kathy Henderson, Attorney Keisha Ware. To Rev. Ron Albertson and Doyle Mackey of Trinity United Methodist Church.

In Florida, to Ms Tomeeke Hayes for her encouragement and support. To Joseph Donoghue, Kathleen McLaurin and the First United Methodist Church of Orlando for assisting refugee families from Somalia and Syria.

To all my siblings, relatives, friends and others who in one way or another shared their support, either spiritually, morally, financially and socially, thank you.

Above all, to the Great Almighty, the giver of life, the author of knowledge and wisdom, for his countless love, protection and provision.

INTRODUCTION

AS A REFUGEE, I would like the world to know that each and every person included under the term "refugee" has a unique narative, one that depicts what people go through when forced to flee from their homeland and deal with traumatizing experiences.

The life stories of many people displaced by war, genocide, and other human rights violations remain unheard. Therefore, it is important to make the world hear the stories directly from the voice of the victims who have experienced them.

The right of every individual to live and prosper must be exercised in every corner of our planet. No mother must have to watch her child die a premature death. No child must be made to live without parents because they were killed in search of food for their children. No daughter must ever be raped or traumatized. No son must be killed because he refuses to bear arms to kill a fellow human being. Let no father be slaughtered in front of his family. The world must say no to an injustice of any kind, anywhere and at any time. As Martin Luther King Jr. rightly said: "Injustice anywhere is a threat to justice everywhere." As children of God, it is important to love and care for one another. It is a commandment from God to love.

The story you are about to read is the true story of a victim of war who traveled through refugee camps in Africa, longing to be accepted in a peaceful country to fulfill the dream of becoming human again.

For many, telling their story can be a healing and liberating experience. Others, like me, would like to use their experiences to contribute something encouraging and inspiring with the purpose of giving hope and fortitude to people facing various kinds of hardship. To preserve the memory that guides our future. To draw attention to social and political injustice. To manifest our gratitude to the several organizations, churches, families, and individuals that have given us the opportunity to make something of our lives.

Just as we have suffered hardship, many of us have been blessed with a tremendous amount of generosity. We might not be economically stable; we might still be suffering from everyday problems. Yet, we have peace, a better way of life and a better chance to exhale. By telling our successful stories, we have the opportunity to express our gratitude to those who have been and continue to be a blessing to us. There is no doubt that there is plenty of evil in the world today, and every time you turn on the TV or read the paper, there is a high chance of learning about another act of violence or chaos in some part of the world, if not in your community. There is more breaking news about evil and less news about acts of generosity.

Regardless of our intentions, one of the most important things when it comes to people who have been affected by war, displacement, and genocide is to decide what to tell and what points to leave out, as our lives could still be affected by some of the things we had to go through unwillingly to save our lives. Of course, revisiting those painful experiences can be an emotional and psychological challenge.

Augustus T. Porter
Florida, United States, 2017

Chapter One

EVERGREEN YARD

Once we accept our limits, we go beyond them.
—Albert Einstein

FOR THOSE OF you who might not be familiar with my country of birth, Liberia is on the West African coast. It is surrounded by Sierra Leone in the west, Guinea in the north, the Ivory Coast in the east and the Atlantic Ocean in the south. Aside from sixteen indigenous languages, the official language is English. The name of our country translates to *land of the free,* something that was difficult to understand when our people learned that at any time there might appear the threat of a merciless massacre waged by neighboring tribes seeking to dominate, torture, and kill men, women, and children.

As the forests on the coastline know how to grow and develop salt-tolerant mangrove trees, adapted to live in harsh conditions, tolerance became a virtue that nature and my parents had inspired in me since my early days. Living in a climate that brought significant rainfall during the rainy season made me appreciate the blessing of free, unpolluted, and abundant water that we learned well how to preserve for times when fresh water would be scarce. This cycle of abundance and lack thereof also taught me that neither of these two aspects of life are permanent. Therefore, I have also learned to flow through every process naturally without resisting it, trusting that if I keep my balance, I will be able to continue evolving through the cyclical movements of life.

I was born in LAMCO Yekepa, Nimba County, Liberia. It was in the early 1980s when my parents moved from Yekepa, a town in northern Nimba County located near the Guinean border – where my siblings also were born – to Voinjama.

I grew up in a household of 10 people, including my mom, dad, four girls and four boys. My sisters are the oldest of my siblings. I was the sixth child.

The Voinjama District is one of six districts located in Lofa County and also close to the Guinean border. It is the capital of Lofa County. There, a wide range of general stores along the main road became a constant attraction for villagers, tourists, business people and my family. My favorite was the ice cream shop. Some of the stores proudly exhibited beautiful quilts and other artistic fabrics, as Liberia possesses a rich history in textile arts and quilting – a very traditional and creative activity brought by the settlers with their sewing and quilting skills. A huge parking station was located in the central plaza to facilitate people taking public cars to different places, including Sierra Leone and the Guinean border, four miles to the north. While the Mano and Gio peoples remained the dominant ethnic groups in the area of Yekepa, most people who lived in Voinjama belonged mainly to the

Lorma and Mandingo tribes – one of West Africa's largest ethno-linguistic groups. Even today many native people practice old indigenous beliefs which, along with Christianity, are the pre-eminent religions, with Muslims making up a small portion of the population.

We moved there to start a new life. My father promoted the change with his leadership disposition. Even though rice farming was the principal occupation of most of the population, my father wanted to cultivate all kinds of crops to allow us to live independently from the trade market. He had so many ideas to develop in this new place: crops, cattle, and a large home with a big yard to provide comfort to his family, relatives, and visitors. I still remember the joy of running, farming and playing under the contrast of a clear blue sky against reddish dirt, surrounded by green grass everywhere. An open nature for my open heart.

All of my siblings and I attended the free Pentecostal School, where the academic excellence was comparable to the best private schools around.

We had a big yard with three houses. There were two small houses – one with one bedroom and a kitchen with a little porch, and the other, where my parents stayed, had two bedrooms, a living room, and a bathroom. The biggest of the three houses had four bedrooms, two bathrooms, a dining room, a living room, a kitchen, a storeroom, and a front and back porch.

I learned many good things from my parents, one of them being generosity. They planted in my siblings and me their humanitarian seed of compassion, respect, and how to behave with the best manners possible at any moment. I learned not to lose my temper, not even during the toughest times, nor to lose focus on my goals. I also learned to establish mental clarity before saying any inconvenient word. I adapted myself to different circumstances, just as the water transforms itself in so many ways without losing its essence – not even for a moment.

My father, Fallah Porter Sr., was a schoolteacher. A man of patience with a kind attitude able to unfold a warm smile at almost any time. He was a disciplinarian, and all the neighbors knew him for that. He learned the art of working with wood, touching it with so much respect and gentleness that everything he did on the wood became a piece of beauty. He taught woodworking at Voinjama Multilateral High School. It was the biggest school in Voinjama at the time. It was not an average high school. There, students were taught technical skills that would enable them to gain employment upon graduation – such things as carpentry, woodworking, auto mechanics, construction, agriculture, and plumbing, among others. My mother, Sarah Porter, also worked at this school as a secretary.

My parents always had relatives, or children of their friends, living with us. Our house was a compassionate shelter for those in need, and I learned how to develop an open heart as a doorway toward a healing space filled with food, water, and warm feelings nourishing everybody's life.

Our father taught us to be aware of and never damage our environment. He told us with so much concern how many endangered species are hunted for human consumption and trade by unscrupulous people who don't care and indiscriminately kill elephants, pygmy hippopotamus, chimpanzees, and other rare animals for food and trade in spite of a ban on the cross-border sale of wildlife. Therefore, an important reservoir of biodiversity is being threatened by cruel and ignorant human beings.

My dad was a conservationist at heart and very determined to be independent and self-sufficient. He was a natural leader, able to inspire in others evolved behaviors – mostly through his impeccable example. As such, he was very hard-working. His vision was to create a land capable of providing us with food carefully cultivated and harvested. He planted his crops, raised his cattle, pigs, sheep, goats, and chickens.

He had multiple fishponds where he raised mostly tilapia and catfish. We never had to buy most of the food we ate on a daily basis. He cultivated it all. We enjoyed our production of bananas, potatoes, plantains, pineapples, collard greens, tomatoes, cabbage, and cassava. He planted enough of those things that when he harvested them, he hired people – sometimes his students and our neighbors – to come and help us harvest everything. Later, he would freely distribute some to the neighbors, and we would still have enough in storage that would keep us going for a while until we were ready for another harvest.

He did the same with animals. We had enough to eat, and this allowed us to share nutritional food with neighbors, as well as to sell food to earn extra income.

My dad duplicated this process with fish. We would harvest a fishpond, and whenever there was a big enough crop, people would come from the community, and all the communities around, to share in it. Lack of food was never a problem.

Along with the importance of hard work, our parents taught us how to be diligent. Most significantly, they taught us the value of education. Even though both of my parents were vocational school graduates – never having gone to college – they always pushed us to seek higher education ourselves. They made sure that we went to the best schools in our region.

At a very young age we proudly learned how to take care of ourselves. We also learned how to be respectful of other people, especially elderly people. We learned how to love other people and how to give to others, particularly those in need. Our parents instructed us to be responsible; each and every one of us had different responsibilities and duties to carry out at home every day. Despite the fact that we had other people living with us, we were not excused from having to do the chores that needed to be done at home. We cleaned our room; we cleaned our house, worked in the yard, washed dishes and clothes; and those that were of age – my sisters, especially – learned how to cook. Mother taught us the art of Liberian cuisine; rice as the food base was combined with our farm produce, with inspired touches of spices like habanero and scotch bonnet chilies. We also spent time cutting the grass to keep our yard neat and beautiful. This work was never a burden, we enjoyed it.

Our yard was always green, and during the dry season when it was sweltering, our dad would make us follow him, pouring water from the well to water the grass. We'd make sure to keep the flowers watered. This is how we became industrious and dependable at a very young age.

Occasionally we would take vacations to other parts of the country, to visit other family members. Sometimes our relatives – especially cousins – came to spend the dry season, when school was closed, with us. There were other times when our schools had events – anniversaries, picnics, soccer and basketball games – when Father allowed us to go and participate. We had so much fun with our friends. Those were good times.

I still long for those days of my youth when at night we played and told stories under the warm starry sky. It highlights my memories of when the cicadas, exalted by the heat of the night, agitated those countless stars that sailed along the darkest skies. We lay back on the ground, amazed by the vast universe above us, with the strange sensation of falling into nameless constellations. I believe that it was in one of those moments that my dream of becoming an airplane pilot haunted me for the first time.

Growing up in my early years of junior high school, I wanted only one thing in life: to become a pilot. To fly an airplane. To earn my living as a pilot. But all of this would change when the civil war erupted and blacked out my skies.

All in all, today I can look back and say that we had a good life before the civil war snatched our dreams, our future, and our innocence. No more stars to fall into. No more places to call home. No more dreams to fly with.

Chapter Two

LETTING GO

When I let go of what I am, I become what I might be.
When I let go of what I have, I receive what I need.

—Lao Tzu

WITH MY DREAM of becoming a pilot torn apart, I didn't know what other things could motivate me to move on with my life. Especially during the civil war, where the experience of having to flee from our land felt like it had rooted out my innocence – a happiness that I didn't know if I would ever be able to achieve again.

Sometimes I wondered: *What if Liberia had never been created?* Could it be possible that the slaves who were freed in the United States after the American Civil War would have been more prosperous, having greater opportunities to develop their lives, if they had stayed in Africa? They had been torn away from their African roots, and unfortunately had become strangers to African culture before arriving in Liberia.

The idea to relocate freed slaves in Africa was inspired by the American Colonization Society (ACS). Then in 1820, free-born African-Americans, along with freed slaves from the United States, came to West Africa to found Liberia. They were called Americo-Liberians and established their community in what is today Monrovia.

Following the dream of *returning home,* thousands of freed American slaves and free-born African-Americans from interdicted slave ships kept coming during the later years. This process led to the formation of several settlements, which ended with the declaration of their independence, becoming the Republic of Liberia on July 26, 1847.

Through America's initiative, Liberia was created with the humanitarian intention of returning the African slaves to "their home" by Robert Finley of New Jersey, who founded the ACS in 1816. Its supporters were Charles Fenton Mercer, Bushrod Washington, Richard Bland Lee, Henry Clay and John Randolph, among others. The group comprised philanthropists, clerics and abolitionists. Their goal to provide free Africans with the opportunity to return to Africa received opposition from most of the free blacks. They saw the move as corny. The Negro Convention movement was a direct response to the formation of the ACS and the Liberia colonization.

In 1818 they denounced the ACS's expansion as an "outrage having no other object in view than the slaveholding interests of the country." This group of African-Americans promoted the freedom of blacks in America and the protection of blacks under laws as any other person in America had. For them, returning to the land they had been removed from for generations was not in their best interest.

Middle-class blacks viewed colonization as a strategy to deport free blacks to Africa to keep them away from taking actions against slavery. On the other hand, some whites felt very strongly that people of African descent should return to Africa.

Solomon Parker, a proponent of colonization, was quoted as saying: "I am not willing that the Man or any of my blacks shall ever be freed to remain in the United States... I am opposed to slavery and also opposed to freeing blacks to stay in our Country and do sincerely hope that the time is approaching when our Land shall be rid of them."

On August 21, 1831, Nat Turner, an enslaved African, led a rebellion of 70 armed slaves and free blacks that resulted in the death of 55 to 65 white neighbors who had enslaved them. The rebels went from one plantation to the other, gathering guns, horses, and freeing other slaves along the way and recruiting others who wanted to join them. Due to the rebellion, Virginia legislators targeted free blacks with a colonization bill that allocated new funding to remove free blacks in addition to a police law that denied them trials by jury and made free blacks convicted of a crime subject to sale and relocation. In vengeance to Turner and others who rebelled, whites organized militias and mobs, killing 200 blacks. Nat Turner was captured. He went to trial on Nov 5, 1831, was convicted and hanged on Nov. 11, 1831, in Jerusalem, Virginia, after hiding himself for two months.

The ACS transported an estimated 16,000 free blacks to Liberia over the period of the 19th century. Many of these

Southern migrants had been freed from enslavement on the condition that they leave the United States.

Slave masters like Gen. Robert E. Lee freed most of his slaves. He offered to undertake the cost of those wanting to be relocated in Liberia like William and Rosabella Burke and their children. Burke attended a seminary in Liberia and became a Presbyterian minister in 1857. William Burke wrote these words to a friend back home a year after he became a Presbyterian minister: *Persons coming to Africa should expect to go through many hardships, such as are common to the first settlement in any new country. I expected it and was not disappointed or discouraged at anything that I met with; and so far from being dissatisfied with the country, I bless the Lord that ever my lot was cast in this part of the earth.*

This higher purpose was only fulfilled for a while, until evil forces developed one of the most merciless, senseless, destructive, demonic, and brutal civil war on the west coast of Africa.

Forced out by the civil war, as my family and I moved to neighboring Guinea as refugees, I was introduced to the computer industry by my cousin Mike Pawa. He taught computer literacy at the Vocational Institute for Refugees in Guinea. If those cruel circumstances had not forced me to leave my dreams of flying professionally, I would never have gotten immersed in computer science. Now, looking back, I realize that this experience has blessed my life. I've become able to integrate many of the technical skills I learned at school into the field of computers. Without a doubt, my new capabilities have opened up more opportunities, enabling me to speak a universal language at any place on the planet where I might be. My job opportunities are much more plentiful everywhere than if I had become a professional pilot – although I still find myself longing to fly.

It was Christmas Eve of 1989 when the civil war began in Liberia. It hit us in Voinjama in July 1990. Even though I was a little child, a feeling of danger haunted me deeply. I woke up that Sunday morning with a heavy weight pressing in my chest. I could hardly catch my breath. I sat and tried to release myself from that anguish. Was it, perhaps, the presage that something terrible would come and change our lives forever? I remember that day when the news broke, saying that the rebels were approaching Voinjama and that everybody must be prepared to flee or to fight. Even though we had not seen any rebels in the area, people in town already knew about them. Their cruel activities were things that our parents had heard about on the radio. Later they would filter what they could tell us.

It all began when Charles Taylor and his National Patriotic Front of Liberia (NPFL) decided to launch an unexpected invasion all along Northern Liberia from his bases in the Ivory Coast. His goal was to overcome the 10 years of dictatorship and corruption created by then-president Samuel Doe. It first started in the northeast of Liberia.

At the beginning, Taylor and his NPFL forces targeted their attacks toward military and government officials. But Doe reacted by killing Gio and Mano civilians – groups linked to

13

supporting Taylor's guerrillas – and the majority of members of this ethnicity fled into neighboring Guinea by the end of 1989. In response to Doe's attacks, Taylor's followers went on to massacre civilians of the Krahn and Mandingo ethnic groups. Unfortunately, elements of the Krahn ethnic group, together with others from the Mandingo, Gio and Mano had committed horrendous atrocities against each other and they were about to pay an extremely painful price – in one of the bloodiest mass murders of the 20th century.

The air around us smelled of danger. Echoes of the pain that was about to come started blowing in the wind.

This war had been largely a struggle of greed for unlimited power among the warring factions. It began as an attempt to end Doe's dictatorship and degenerated into ethnic massacres, followed by hatred as each faction fought from a vengeful spirit. As a consequence, the rebellion developed unrestrained murders on a massive scale.

Since the eruption of the civil war, most families listened very intently every day to the radio. In that part of the country, in Voinjama, we had no access to television, so our news was brought to us mostly by the Liberian Broadcasting System and the BBC.

The elderly people, like my parents, their friends, relatives, and other people, would listen to the news and have long talks about what was happening at that time in the country. Sometimes they told us what was going on. Other times we just heard the conversations of older folks talking about the tragedy to come at any moment.

As the rebels captured most parts of the country, things began to feel horrifying to us. The closer they got, the more terrified we became. By July of 1990 we had about 50 people at home. A lot of family members came from other counties, where the rebels had captured many civilians, and were approaching fiercely toward us in Voinjama. At this point, we had a lot of people. My father made arrangements for others to stay in other areas of the same community. Facing the worst, our feelings of vulnerability knocked us down, as we had never imagined this could happen to us. Even though we had not heard a single gunshot nearby, the atmosphere around us was dreadful. Just by seeing displaced people in huge numbers walking hundreds of miles looking for safety, made me feel how our *evergreen* home would be devastated by the horror of a merciless war.

In an instinctive act of self-rescue, I ran to the far back yard to calm my spirit around our peaceful animals. My mother looked at me through the window with compassionate eyes. I walked through the corral, and every living being seemed to be fine – not sensing the approaching danger. And I loved these animals as if they were members of my family. I had rabbits given to me by a friend of my dad. They were my proud possession and I was very, very sad to leave them. They were so beautiful. But I had to let them go now. The cattle stared at me with ruminating eyes. In a full deep breath, I tried to absorb our evergreen land to keep it with me in my memory forever. An ominous silence wrapped every-thing. I remained suspended in that stillness, longing to find

15

refuge in something bigger than the determined strength of my mother's arms. Would this be the end?

The sun began to fall, and with it any hope of surviving the ferocious attacks of the bloody minds.

Chapter Three

THE SPIRITUAL SIDE OF EPILEPSY

I am about to discuss the disease called "sacred,"
epilepsy. Its origin, like that of other diseases,
lies in heredity. The fact is that the cause of this
affliction, like the more serious diseases gener-
ally, is the brain.
—Hippocrates of Cos, 500 B.C.

MY FATHER WAS the son of a local Kissi chief of the Hundoni village from the Foya district of Lofa County, Liberia. At the age of 15, his older brother, George Pawa, took him away from his parents to attend school in the Bolahun, Kolahun District. After graduating from high school, my father studied in a vocational school to become a carpenter. It was then that he moved to LAMCO and met my mother.

Pursuing his dream of creating a better life, he received a government scholarship and went to Japan to master his studies in woodworking – something for which he had developed a natural talent. His personal touch on the wood made it appear exquisite and valuable. He always had a great respect for nature in all of its forms. I can also say that he treated the wood as if it were still breathing inside the tree – a unique spirit that had to be honored, a beauty that would never be damaged in spite of the years.

LAMCO was the place where our family's story began. I lived there happily with my parents and siblings. Even though life in LAMCO was perfect for all of us, better work opportunities motivated my father to move the family to Voinjama. My mother remained in LAMCO with her youngest child until she gave birth to my youngest brother, whose name would be Fallah.

I was still very young when my father took us to Voinjama. I remember how much I missed the comfort we used to have in LAMCO, where we had easy access to electricity, paved roads, and a better hospital. Voinjama, instead, was just the opposite. No paved roads. No electricity. A very poor water source. My dad had to boil water from the well, treat it with chlorine, and store it in a container to keep it fresh. That is how we would get our drinking water when there was no running water available. We must have had the perfect Guardian Angel to help us survive the threats of severe epidemic diseases such as malaria, and tuberculosis, among others.

I have always admired the temperament of my parents and how they managed the most difficult moments with us. I admired their wisdom for nourishing us with the most essential nutrient any child should ever receive – unconditional love.

In spite of the lack of electricity, the unsaved water, the unpaved streets, and the risk of catching severe endemic diseases, poverty was never an issue in our family. We were wealthy in our values and love. My mother and father were very skilled parents – trustworthy and committed to the wellbeing of their eight children. Eight children who never missed any part of formal education both in schools and at home. Both academic and humanitarian. I took these values for granted when I was a child. Now, as an adult, I realize how grateful I am for having had these two people as my parents.

My younger brother, Fallah, began suffering from severe seizures in his early days. His illness became a very painful and disturbing experience for all of us.

In spite of his sickness, Fallah grew up to be bigger and taller than most kids his age. His dark and curly hair, combined with his vivacious eyes, would perfectly frame and enhance his presence wherever he went. Although our parents had always encouraged gentle manners in all of their eight children, it didn't take long for Fallah to develop a hostile attitude toward others who offended him. None of his friends dared to mess with him. He never shrank against difficulties. Facing challenges was one of his most enjoyable games. He perceived himself as an honorable warrior, an invincible force that had the ability to defeat even the most ferocious adversaries.

As much as he enjoyed playing with other children, he would react aggressively when he felt that someone had offended him. He used to fight with everybody. His peers became very cautious when dealing with him. He wasted no time in slapping anyone, including our parents, when he felt aggrieved.

19

Observing Fallah's behavior, I wondered if the unexpected seizures were an eruption of some unconscious anger that took over his personality. We feared the possibility of his death during the epileptic attacks.

I wondered if epilepsy also had a spiritual side, that for some inexplicable reason had been poisoned and needed to be released from the darkest of energies?

How I wished that we had had another cure for epilepsy aside from daily medication. We were all trained to give Fallah his medicine every day. Often, he got frustrated and tired of taking pills. He rejected them. We would try every way we could think of to persuade him to take his medication, but at times it was very difficult. On most of these occasions it would take more than a sibling to administer his dose. We would have to let our parents know, and they would make him take his medicine. We all suffered for him. We all knew how difficult it was for him to deal with the side effects of seizure medication. He didn't like to experience tiredness, dizziness, or any discomfort. But medication was the only way.

My parents were very persistent in making sure that Fallah was able to receive the best treatment available in the country. They took him to every hospital, specialist, clinic, and doctor that was recommended to them by other doctors, family members, and friends across the country. His condition was on and off. There were times when he would have 10 seizures in one day. He'd have a seizure at school or when playing with friends. Day and night, his epileptic attacks wouldn't leave him at peace. Only once or twice would he have seizures at night and go to school the next morning. Because of this, he slept in our parents' bed with them. Most of his seizures occurred at night.

We also noticed that he would have a lot of seizures during the new moon. Would it be possible, perhaps, that if the moon influences water – as it does the tides in the ocean – and water, being an indispensable element in our human body, could the body be affected by the cycle of the moon as well? I have so many questions surrounding the causes of epilepsy.

Even though we grew up in a country surrounded by tribal animistic religions where the world of spirits, hidden in nature and inanimate figures, became the supernatural medicine able to release people from evil conditions, my parents only chose to believe in the scientific approach to fighting any disease. They never followed any witchcraft practices. This behavior kept my siblings and I from developing any curiosity surrounding spiritual beliefs other than those coming from our Christian Church.

Any illness, whether light or severe, had to be treated by orthodox medical doctors – or, on very few occasions, my mother would explore the possible benefits of herbal medicine – something that my father didn't support. Instead, he promoted the practice of praying, suggested by our church, but even more so he promoted all of the advice, treatment, and guidance from medical doctors. But prayers and fasting were the only other approaches that he believed in to contribute alongside the cure of ordinary medical treatments.

My mother, *the doctor mother,* as we used to call her, had her emergency cabinet at home filled with prescribed medicine for epilepsy along with chloroquine, aspirins, penicillin, a huge range of vitamins, bandages, alcohol – everything ready to keep us safe before going to the hospital if circumstances required special attention.

On the bright side, there were times when Fallah would go for three months without any seizures. These were the happiest moments for all of us, especially our parents. Because of the inconsistency of his seizures, we would always keep an eye on him. The moment that we noticed he was not around, we would go and search for him. It was very annoying for my brother to see us coming for him when he was playing with friends. Without asking for permission, we would interrupt the game and bring him home, or move their game to somewhere where we could watch.

It was always a sad experience to see him fall on hard surfaces, like the ground or concrete floor. Still today the bitterness of those moments doesn't easily leave my memories. There were moments in which we were able to prevent his falls. We learned that seizure attacks showed signs before they happened. A typical sign was when he would stare out in a direction without blinking. When this occurred while he was standing, we would run to protect him from falling before the convulsion occurred. Unless someone happened to know that he suffered from these convulsive attacks, they would never realize that he had epilepsy. Fallah looked very healthy, energetic, active, and motivated.

He took phenobarbital most of his life. My parents even tried the advice of an herbalist. One after the other, each naturalist doctor promised that they could cure him. They were all recommended and highly accredited, but none was able to heal my brother. They all came from different places with different backgrounds and styles of administering their treatment. My dad was always very critical of herbal treatment. My mom, on the other hand, was always very convinced that they would be able to cure her son. I don't remember all of the various treatments, but I do remember one herbalist placing a bracelet-like thing around his wrist and instructing us not to take it off until my brother was well. This doctor requested that my parents bring him a tortoise. They paid for one and the herbalist killed it, cooked its meat with a special herb, and made it into a stew. He told my parents to add a certain amount into each of my brother's meals for a few days. My brother did not like it; he said it was tasteless. My dad did not like the idea that it had to be kept and given to my brother for more than two days.

Most herbalist treatment looked unhealthy, and for this reason, my dad was always concerned that it would make my brother sicker rather than curing him. However, the referrals always convinced him to accept it, or to at least try it, to see if it would work. Like any other parent who would take the risk if that was what was needed to cure their child, he did. Unfortunately, none of the treatments worked. He rejected some herbalist treatments; others he did not want to continue.

But it was not just that my younger brother suffered from epilepsy since my parents moved us to Voinjama. He was the second one in the family. My oldest sister, Onike, was the first to fall seriously ill in the family. She also had terrible and traumatic attacks from her nervous system. I was ten years younger than she and at that time I wasn't very aware of her disease. Nevertheless, I do remember her falling seriously ill one night. She fell unconscious and foam was bubbling out of her mouth. Her eyes were wide open, stretched in one direction like someone who had fainted. Onike looked very pale, as if she were dead. She became stiff and lay straight on her back. My parents propped her head up with pillows to prevent her from choking on her own saliva. They pulled ice from the freezer and placed it on her head. People were coming and going in and out of the house as my siblings and I cried, thinking the worst. A few minutes later she was placed in the back seat of a car and rushed to the hospital.

Now as an adult, I have learned that my oldest sister was mentally ill. She too was placed on medication. Her disease didn't manifest itself as often nor as severely as our brother's seizures. Hers was usually triggered when she wanted something that she didn't get. After being under deep stress she would start behaving abnormally. No one understood her better than my dad. He had the ability to knock her out of it. He knew what provoked her illness; therefore, he let her get away with things that we would get in trouble for.

Like Fallah and Onike, I also suffered from a brief period of seizures. There were times when I had convulsions to a lesser degree. I felt helpless and very scared. I started wondering where these undesirable genes might have come from. What was the message? With great devotion and courage my parents went through the anguish of helping us to get rid of this plight.

We took refuge in scientific medicine and prayers from our Christian beliefs. But what if we had overlooked another path that could have provided us with a definitive cure?

Churches like the Aladura Church – "Prayer People" – fasted, prayed, and performed various rituals while my mom would stay with my brother at the church. This behavior was very scary for me. We never practiced any kind of rituals in our house. We learned to associate rituals with witchcraft activities that might bring diabolical consequences. We didn't want to know, so we knew nothing about witchery.

We went to Christian schools and our parents allowed us to attend any church of our choice. I frequented most churches – Pentecostal, Baptist, Methodist, Episcopal, Seventh Day Adventist, Assembly of God and Catholic churches. We knew that when someone walked by the river chanting, or would go to the ocean at night to pray, we needed to stay away from those practices.

At the Aladura Church they would wear white garments, walk around barefoot, burn incense, and roll on the dusty ground while praying. It was very strange to see my mom bringing my brother into those rituals.

The longing to find my brother a cure didn't last. Things went beyond our control and his condition became worse.

I understand my mother now, as I understood her then. Living with a beloved child who is traumatically trapped in an illness that has treatment but no cure must have been devastating for her. About a week later my dad moved Fallah to another town. They went to Zorzor, a city in Lofa County, which at that time had one of the best hospitals in the region. Fallah's condition improved considerably, and they never returned to the Aladura church.

As for me, as a kindergarten student at William Brown Kindergarten School, I received great care and love from my teacher, Miss Nyanly.

I was smart, neat, quiet, and well behaved. I had dark gums, a big head with a wide afro. Miss Nyanly knew about my seizures. Therefore, she would help keep an eye on me when I was in school. My disorder was entirely different from my brother's; I had way fewer seizures than he did. I remember having three seizures between kindergarten and the fifth grade. In kindergarten, I had a seizure while trying to get over the wall of the school balcony, which was about five feet up from the ground. I was among a group of my peers trying to quickly climb over the balcony as a shortcut to get from one building to another, where we were going for a school event. I fell and began to convulse. Unlike with my brother Fallah, very few people knew I had any disorder. My friends and the school staff thought that I was dying. I was immediately taken to the Voinjama Telewoyan Hospital. My mother was informed right away. By the time she arrived at the hospital, I was already recovering. A few days later I was well and ready to go back to school. From that point on, I was banned by my mother from climbing anything.

The second episode was at home; I was already down with a fever, so I had the attention of my parents and everybody in the house to protect me from a fall. This time I had a seizure in my mother's arms. I will never forget how much garlic and donut grease (Shea Butter) she rubbed on me with before calling the nurse who treated me at home.

The third episode occurred when I was in the fifth grade. At this time in my life, I was a true boy. Soccer was at the top of my list of interests. We had a 30-minute break for recess every day at school. On this fateful day, I played soccer with my friends during recess. The bell was ringing, calling us back to class. My friends and I stopped playing and ran back to class. They all ran into the classroom. I sat on the floor against the side of a long hallway in front of three classrooms: the fourth, fifth and sixth grades. The last thing I remember before I had my seizure and fell backward, hitting my head on the concrete floor, was my best friend and seatmate Francis Saygbeh calling me by my middle name: Tamba, Tamba... I did not respond. He started running toward me, but I hit the floor before he arrived. This time around, the school nurse treated me on campus at the school's clinic. After treatment, I was taken to my mom's work. It was the last time I remember having a full seizure that resulted in a fall.

This time, my mom decided to try something very different and strange; she took me to her relative, Ruth Bimba, who lived closer to my mother's work than we did. We called her Sis Ruth. As soon as we arrived there, my mother explained what had happened to me and in no time Sis Ruth implemented everything she needed to assist me as fast as she could. She pulled out a bucket, filled it with cold water in front of her house, and placed it on the stairs – very long stairs leading from the street to the front of the house. She lived on a major street. My mother undressed me quickly down to my underwear. As if time were running against us, she immediately emptied the bucket full of cold water all over me. I will never forget being showered on the street. Along with the cold bath she rubbed me with garlic, alcohol, and a homemade blend to break the fever.

Being sick in my parent's house brought lots of benefits. When we were sick, we got to eat the best of everything; it was one of the few times when we could ask for anything we wanted. We were treated like princes and princesses. We would even get new clothes. Depending on what the illness was, we would get new robes, thin tops, socks, towels, or new sheets. As a grown-up I still use some of her special treatments for minor illnesses.

I must say that having experienced some seizures myself, it is like being suspended in the eternal. One slips out of control into a terrifying abyss. Anything, even a sudden unexpected death in epilepsy, could happen in just seconds. You are at the mercy of unknown forces, fearing the worst. Your nervous system collapses, leading to convulsions, struggling, trembling, shuddering, and other disturbing epileptic activities.

Over the years I have observed these seizures and would compare them to the rhythms of the Voodoo drums – to frantic tribal dances which have been practiced for millennia in Africa. Where people would yield to uncontrollable forces, allowing their consciousness to go away as if the mind were an unworthy gift of life. The common factor between convulsions and altered states of consciousness released in some particular tribal dances lies in the fact that the energy flowing through the body exceeds the ability of the brain to handle and channel it, resulting in seizures and exhaustion of the nervous system.

Today, seeing everything from afar, I can understand that there might have been genetic factors that had unleashed inevitable seizures in us, maybe, along with other potential causes of epilepsy that are still beyond scientific explanation.

Researchers from different disciplines have found at least four possible sources of seizures: physical illness, emotional trauma, demonic activities, and a desire to escape an unwanted reality. I still wonder which one of these could have been the cause of our suffering, or if it perhaps could have been a combination of all of them.

Chapter Four

HOW PARADISE TURNED INTO HELL

...The boys are trained to kill, even if
they have to kill their mothers.
– Charles Taylor, to his child soldiers
—Liberia,
First Civil War
1989-1996

IF I HAD to compare the cruelty of the rebels to a monstrous human entity, I would describe it as a unit of ghoulish behaviors.

I can't remember when most of the events occurred, and yet I can still remember the feelings. I still remember what happened as if a turbulent nightmare were running through my mind and my spirit every once in a while. Releasing these sorrows is hard. Perhaps sharing them here will help me and others to feel consoled someday.

People had heard rumors about the rebels approaching Voinjama, and the news of what was happening in Monrovia was appalling. They learned that many businesses had been shut down there, along with several government offices.

Some Liberians came to the realization that it would soon be necessary to leave the country. The news on the radio confirmed that the rebels were fighting in nearby cities. They were heading toward us. Although the government of Samuel Doe – and those who preceded him – had triggered Liberia toward a bloody civil war, the rebels who came with the excuse of liberating our country ended up immersing us in one of the cruelest wars that had ever been known.

Anticipating the danger that soon would flagellate Voinjama, my father had organized everything for us to leave the city immediately for the land of his ancestors, where he was born. He wanted to protect us from the rebels who had indiscriminately slaughtered civilians in every town and village that they had passed through. His plan was that my mother, together with my siblings and I, would travel to Foya, near the Guinean border, to be sheltered at his brother's house until every possible harm had subsided. He himself would stay at home to finish some business and would join us as soon as possible.

Neither my father nor my mother wanted to make us feel afraid or unprotected, but I sensed that something terrible was about to happen. The news on the radio was grim. We didn't have much time left. The rebels would bring only blood and despair. I could see how my mother tried to hide her fears and channel them into hurried preparations for our immediate departure. We had a long journey ahead. She knew what might be waiting for us along those roads full of threats and possible death. But staying at home wouldn't have been an option – quite the opposite.

- We better hurry!
- We must hurry!
- Let's hurry!

"Hurry!" became a stressful sound coming from my mother and my elder siblings. I was finishing packing when Steven, my brother-in-law at that time, arrived with his little blue car. We all tried to fit into his five-passenger sedan– my mother, my seven siblings, and I. After several attempts we shrank, and were forced to sit on each other's laps. My father pressed on the back door until it finally closed. It was time to depart. Even though we were leaving our old life behind, there was no room for nostalgia. The fear of imminent death was consuming our minds.

In an attempt to hold onto their last moment together, my mother extended her hand out to my father. He held it with the strength of a lover who would always be there for us.

The sun was giving up its light, as we did with the life we used to have. From the back seat I turned to wave goodbye to my dad. A reddish dust was moving around him. I didn't know if that would be the last time I would see him again. I remember swallowing a tear that I couldn't release from my eyes. I have never seen my father cry; that is probably not what a real man is made of. My stomach was aching, and I saw his figure growing smaller and smaller the farther I went.

While we were fleeing from Voinjama, pressed in the seats of my brother-in-law's small car, I could see, across the curtain of dust that lifted the car, the horror and suffering of those running away on foot, carrying their essential belongings along with their children and animals. Some eyes, enlarged by sadness, looked at me as we passed by. So much would I have liked to have had a place to rescue them all away to, to escape the possibility of death that awaited them if the rebels arrived before they were able to get away – I could also see part of the history we were leaving behind.

I was just a child when the rebels were approaching Voinjama. That small city that served as the capital of Lofa County was so vulnerable and unable to resist the ferocious attack that was coming. Everything that was about to happen in our little paradise was unknown and unexpected to me. Although I'd listened to the adults sharing their concerns surrounding what the radio was continuously broadcasting, I had no idea of the magnitude of the violence that would change our lives forever. Now I believe that the people of Voinjama could not have been fully aware of what was about to happen either, except for those who slowly began to flee from an inevitable and bloody extermination.

What I learned later on as an adult allowed me to see a broader picture of the complex circumstances that had brought us toward an irremediable hell.

By the end of the 16th century, the Europeans developed the idea of an infamous human traffic which soon would be the most common commerce. The inhuman slave trading provoked the loss of approximately 20 million African lives. It severely damaged the continent by removing from their roots young women and men who were the most productive workers of the land. Not only did this create a shortage of people dedicated to producing for their country, but slavery left resentment and irreconcilable hostilities between the different tribes.

Around the time of the first Liberian civil war, this intertribal enmity became the basis of a deadly hatred easing the way to justifying human extermination.

After Liberia suffered this heated civil war in the late 1970s, the opposition to the Americo-Liberian government led to a murderous military coup. As a consequence of this rebellion, the Krahn leader, Samuel Doe, became the new head of state in 1980 – the first Liberian president who belonged to an indigenous group. During this time the Krahn people, who had previously been a disparaged and primitive tribe, received a place of honor and respect within Doe's government due to his favoritism toward them. With their rise in status during Doe's government, many Krahn people moved to the capital, Monrovia.

The Krahn people, originally came from Northeast Africa at the beginning of the 16th century, fleeing persecution and seeking better living conditions. During this time, the commerce in slaves began to attract tribes ready to get rid of their enemies, whom they kidnapped and sold. Though refusing to enslave their own tribe members, they nevertheless served as local traders on the coast of Liberia, negotiating deals with the Western slave market.

In the latter part of the 20ᵗʰ century, after decades of abusive dictatorship, those in exile – along with members of other indigenous groups – began organizing their militant forces to defeat Doe and the Krahn people.

All through the 1990s, tribal divisions among the various ethnic groups became evident in the political field. During Samuel Doe's dictatorship he favored his own indigenous group and persecuted the rest of the population. Due to this conflict and the rampant corruption of Doe's government, Liberia lost the economic support of the United States, which spurred the cutoff of foreign aid. The state of his regime had exacerbated already bad conditions, making life intolerable for the various ethnic groups.

Charles Taylor, an Americo-Liberian, took advantage of these tribal tensions for his own purpose. As soon as he became the leader of the National Patriotic Front of Liberia (NPFL) in 1990, he immediately brutalized the country, transforming it into one of the grisliest war zones ever seen in West Africa.

In late 1989, Charles Taylor recruited and trained various non-Krahn peoples, thousands of Gio and Mano groups to erase the Krahn people. As he crossed through Nimba County, he continued recruiting young Gio and Mano men and children to increase his troops. Many of those children had to accept becoming "child soldiers" even if they didn't want to. Otherwise, they would receive terrible reprisals against their own lives and those of their families. With them, and another ill-prepared militia, Taylor invaded Liberia from the Ivory Coast on Christmas Eve of 1989, and began attacking Krahn civilians in Nimba and Grand Gedeh counties. Through this invasion there began a series of wars which tore the country to pieces. His forces massacred and destroyed entire communities as they moved forward, increasing the fear and hatred that had already existed between the different indigenous groups. Among the other groups that were slaughtered were the Mandingo people, who mainly occupied Voinjama city, where I lived at that time with my family and relatives.

The pre-existing rivalries among the various ethnic groups established an accessible and willing source for recruiting resentful tribes. Hatred and revenge motivated each soldier to cruelly murder innocent civilians, either because the victim belonged to an indigenous group perceived as the enemy, or because the soldier suspected that they belonged to one of these groups.

What began as a war to liberate the country from crime and an abusive dictatorship became an atrocious battle between competing factions. They fought to gain domination and power over anybody that they suspected of conspiring against the rebels – and from there, just anybody. Their depraved behaviors created an insane atmosphere characterized by merciless vandalism, rape, torture, and murder of unarmed civilians of all ages. They used child soldiers to kill, rape, slaughter and mass murder with an unimaginable level of violence that was fueled by the malicious administering of drugs. Very soon, the Liberian civil war had forgotten its purpose of liberating the country from a ruthless dictatorship, becoming an eternal hell.

Nothing could ever have justified the pain that still today spills over our bloodstained land. A vicious war fueled by resentment and revenge that started for political reasons, went further and detonated the rivalry between the tribes who allied with the government and those who supported the rebels. An unstoppable monster was responsible for an endless massacre that shattered an unsuspecting civilian population. Entire villages were left emptied. Families were ripped apart – mutilated, devastated, and slaughtered. Hundreds of thousands of lives were lost under a merciless power. Millions of Liberians fled, seeking refuge in neighboring countries, and my family was on its way to join them.

Every time the rebels went to attack a town, they would surround it and begin shooting big weapons. One of the weapons that everybody was familiar with was an RPG, a rocket-propelled grenade launcher, which fired explosive rockets. They would launch the big weapons first, and then start the shooting. Everybody was confused and in a state of panic. They'd shoot all around the town to create terror and chaos. Nobody knew where to go to be safe. They killed women, children, and elders without mercy.

We had known of that strategy before they hit Voinjama. That is why we couldn't wait and witness it ourselves. When they came to Voinjama, they would launch the same kind of organized attack. They would circle the whole town and herd everybody to be terrified in the soccer field of the public school.

Among the primary targets to be killed by Charles Taylor's forces were the people of the Mandingo tribe, whose population was very large in Voinjama. They became one of the most victimized groups during the war. Nobody of any ethnicity was safe from the slaughter that these savages would bring.

Four days after we arrived in Foya, the rebels took over Voinjama. My father was there, trusting that nothing could happen to him. Sometimes I believe that the spirit of a great warrior must have grown inside him since his childhood, or perhaps it was born with him. He would remain calm when faced with the worse of difficulties, without manifesting any disturbed feeling. When others were trembling, he was sustained by the courage of an inner power that I had always admired. It was as if that power gave him the ability to become invisible against the attack of a blinded madness. No savage could have smelled any fear in my father. He had the virtue of turning feelings of distress into an energy and was capable of getting through the most adverse struggles. Next to him I felt protected by an invincible force. Everything could have fallen apart around us except that the roof that had always been held up by my father's strength. Even knowing his exceptional fortitude, I still wonder how he could have survived what he had witnessed when the rebels came to destroy life in Voinjama.

My father saw the rebels requesting various people to leave their homes and head to the open soccer field of a public school. One by one, they left their homes and walked toward a certain death. Some might have harbored the hope that they would not die that day, or ever during the rebel's occupation. Others might have sensed that an inevitable extermination would occur that day, or another. They walked from their homes to the field where they were all surrounded by rebels.

Somehow, my father managed to make his way back home, but not without feeling so much sorrow for all of his fellow Lofians. Many had died, and those who survived had been terribly tortured. Nobody from my dad's immediate neighborhood was killed that day.

Still today it is hard to believe how my dad was able to survive those three months he remained in Voinjama. Those were horrendous times for the entire population. All offices and businesses were immediately closed when the rebels took over Voinjama. After they had mercilessly massacred families – just out of suspicion that they could have belonged to a targeted ethnicity – anyone could be horribly killed using whatever excuse.

The rebels looted everything: hospitals, schools, government offices, businesses, properties from which people had fled, cars, radio stations, and police headquarters. The only cars running were owned by the rebels. They enslaved everyone whom they hadn't killed. They forced the civilians to collect food and stock it in their warehouses. They forced women and young girls to cook for them every day. At this time everybody was in a great state of panic. The most dangerous time was during the first few days after the rebels arrived. The worse the atrocity, the more they felt empowered by their sadistic behaviors.

Anything the rebels considered to be a contradiction to their purpose would pass as a good reason for someone to be killed, sometimes after being subjected to bloody tortures that only a monstrous mind could commit. What was even more terrifying was that all the rebels shared this monstrous way of thinking. They were nothing less than the evil manifestation of a monstrous collective mind. Those criminal behaviors would make people talk about them. They became both famous and infamous. They loved to be perceived as "wicked commandos."

The rebels would walk around the neighborhood carrying their guns openly. They would loot anything they saw on their way and would take possession of any house they wanted to live in. If anyone was in the house they would throw them out – or kill them – and move in themselves. The violent behavior became contagious among the rebels. A competition began to see who could dare to be the cruelest. In this manner, they fed their hunger for revenge and sadism.

There were no phones available to use to check up on relatives, friends, or neighbors. Occasionally my father would walk a long way to some neighbors' houses. Most of the time they would listen to the radio, talk quietly about the situation, and discuss whether they could continue to stay or if they would have to leave, even though leaving would also put their lives at risk.

As soon as the time of greatest tension gradually diminished, my dad dared to begin taking care of what was left of our farm. He was also able to go to the fishpond close to the house. But he couldn't do any business; there was nothing to sell nor a customer to buy anything. The entire town had turned into a wasteland. The rebels had robbed all they could and devastated everything in their path.

Even though my father lived under constant danger from the rebels, he dared to go on the local radio station to inform us that the rebels had taken Voinjama and that where ever we might be, he wanted us to stop and not to go across the border to Sierra Leone, which was our initial destination before stopping in our village, Hundoni.

Mom and Dad, 2001 Wheaton IL.

Chapter Five

THE KISSI PEOPLE

ALL ALONG THE way to the land of our ancestors, we saw people walking desolately toward an uncertain future. Mothers carrying their young ones on their backs – some had babies in their arms, and some brought suitcases and bags of their belongings on their heads, walking for days and nights to safety and away from the rebels. Everything was sorrowful.

Our journey was exhausting. Not all the roads were in good condition, and the heat didn't make the trip easy. We were heading toward my uncle's home in Foya, and we knew that if things became dreadful, our father had instructed Steven to continue across the border into Sierra Leone.

The people we kept finding on our way were countless. Hundreds and hundreds of families, babies, children, the elderly, the sick – all walking, drained and hopeless. They had scarcely eaten and seemed to be severely dehydrated. What once were their clothes were now rags. What once were their dreams were now a hint of life barely sustained by a weak breath. They had become a shred of what they once had been.

I thought that in the midst of the tragedy, we were still lucky to be in a vehicle.

How could I ever forget this? What could have produced such an outbreak of bloody madness? Had the devil not been satisfied enough after punishing our country with ethnic rivalries, lack of vital resources and infrastructure, poverty, corruption, and people being atrociously uprooted from their land and sold as slaves...? How is it possible that children of my age, and even younger, had committed such merciless atrocities against innocent people of all ages – raping, torturing, murdering? Could it perhaps be that those cults to demons, practiced for thousands of years in my country, had unleashed the most ferocious forces of evil to manifest themselves in the spirits of these child soldiers and their chiefs? Because what they had done was the work of heartless beings, it was difficult to consider them humans.

After endless hours of driving, we arrived in Foya. Our uncle was there, opening the car door as well as our hopes of surviving – even though we didn't know for how long. I remember his smiling face – the shine in his eyes. He made me feel protected. His home was spacious and warm. But we were not allowed to get comfortable. We spent the night in Foya, but we did not stay there. It wasn't safe. In the morning, my uncle told my mother that he would be forced to leave Foya and flee to Sierra Leone. His wife belonged to the Krahn tribe – the ethnicity from which President Doe had come from, and therefore they'd been persecuted and killed by the rebels. His house wouldn't be a safe place for us to stay either. Everything had been moving so fast. Nothing was stable anymore.

That day, before fleeing to Sierra Leone with his wife and children, my uncle made all the arrangements for us to stay in a secure shelter. We needed to move fast to the village of my grandparents. While he was saying goodbye, he couldn't hide his sadness and fears. Tomorrow, later, the future – everything was losing perspective. None of us could have known what was waiting for us ahead. That was, perhaps, one of the most terrifying feelings I could have ever experienced. I ran to my uncle and hugged him. I needed to breathe his strength, to feel his heart – his life. He was my father's blood, mine too. I didn't want him to leave us. He embraced me too, and I sighed. My mother put her arm around my shoulder and took me to the car. I didn't turn back this time. I haven't seen him since. We headed to the Village of the Kissi people – from where all of our family belongs. A place where my dad was born and lived until he was 15 years old.

I arrived at Hundoni with my mother and all my siblings. It was right after midday and the heat was extreme in the village of my ancestors. Thirst, exhaustion, and hunger were not able to dispel our fears.

My father's family was so happy to shelter us. My uncle Fayia Miller hugged me with so much tenderness that he was capable of washing every trace of anguish that consumed me since we had fled possible death. There was no war, nowhere, within his arms. And my grandma, she ran toward me spreading my father's smile. She took my cheeks in her hands and kissed me with tears rolling over her shiny face. One of my uncles put his hands on my shoulder and invited us to come into the house. As we walked in, the smell of home welcomed us. Grandmother's food was waiting for us on the large table that my father had crafted. We sat and ate as if nothing was happening in the country. Nobody said a word about anything harmful. My uncle blessed the moment we arrived there, along with me too.

My grandmother, who was very hardworking and loving, was the head wife of my grandfather, who had multiple wives. He picked her as his head wife because she was caring, hardworking and beautiful. She had very soft, dark skin and big strain hair. She had small legs like her oldest son – my uncle, George Pawa – had. She had four biological kids and my dad, Fallah Porter, was the youngest.

She used to call her boys by their last name, and when she called my dad "Porter," it sounded like "Kpanya Coubah," a traditional dish from my tribal group, the Kissi. She made it with potato leaves cooked in red oil and it was eaten with white rice. She carefully washed the leaves and placed them on top of the rice, allowing all the ingredients to steam together. Once everything was cooked, she would remove only the leaf and pepper from the top of the rice, put it in another pot, and use the back of a wooden cooking spoon to mash the leaves and pepper as much as she could so it would look like rubgreen. My grandmother made this dish very well. It was very affordable, easy, and quick to cook compared to cassava leaf or other Liberian dishes.

I found a great contrast from the life we used to have in Voinjama. Everything was different in the place of my ancestors. Even the lack of comfort I was accustomed to having in Voinjama did not seem to bother me too much. Their traditions and ancient beliefs had captured my senses. Circumstances had pushed into a familiar journey – nothing I was expecting to experience. Especially those moments of fascinating discoveries where nature itself was exalted as a manifestation of magical worlds.

The Kissi were among the tribes who had been taken to be sold as slaves. They were obliged to walk hundreds of miles through jungles and other dangerous roads toward the coastal towns, where their lives would be torn apart, in most cases, forever. Their capacity to recover from devastation would inspire in me a sense of courage that would run through my blood eternally. Today I learned that psychology named this behavior "resilience," defined as the ability to successfully adapt to life tasks in the face of social disadvantage or highly adverse conditions.

I belong to the Kissi ethnic group of Liberia because both my parents are Kissi – from the Foya District in Lofa County. When I look back, I can see my ancestors traveling several thousands of years back in Liberia, in its neighboring lands and far beyond Kenya.

My father was born in Hundonin. He was the son of a Kissi chief who lived in the village of Hundoni. Except for my father, who was monogamous and only married my mother, most fathers in the villages had multiple wives with a different set of kids each. Each mother was responsible for her children, and the father bore the overall responsibility. He spent less time with each individual child, but the head wife's kids enjoyed the most time with their father in most cases. In the case of my Uncle Miller, he had a separate house for all of the other wives, at least five of them, and he and his head wife would live in the same house. Each wife had her own room. When the kids were young, they would stay with the mother in the same room. Grown kids stayed in separate places, mostly grouped by genders. Boys usually stayed together and girls together as well.

There are many small villages ruled by chiefs, and most of them are tucked inside groves of mango, orange, banana, cocoa or kola trees. Being primarily farmers, their life is mostly dedicated to the cultivation of rice, in addition to manioc, sugar cane, coffee, and cocoa. I belong to this agrarian culture that lives in the neighboring region of Guinea, Liberia, and Sierra Leone. The Kissi are organized into villages of about 150 or more people each and are located in clearings. It didn't take a lot of time until I felt in tune with the culture of my ancestors. When it did happen, an ancestral call shook me deeply.

No one ever needed to hide his or her age because for the Kissi being an elder is an honor, and the communities are therefore led by a chief and the elderly. Their big eyes, so black and brilliant, are a cult to the innocence. Everything amazes them. Everything surprises them. They believe in everything. Even a fish can bring them messages, and this is something that still today captivates me. Kissi people do not question the subtle guidance coming from the spirits of nature. Some oracles, as those of prosperity, can be experienced from the fishes they nurse in their sacred rivers.

Some people tend to think that those who live in tropical places prefer to be idle due to the heat, or because they have everything they need from nature, or perhaps a combination of the two. For the Kissi people that is not the case. They love to work as if it were a constant motivation to be alive. The pulse of life is consistently beating in their heart as much as in their muscles and blood. They need not the melody but the temperamental force of that drumming rhythm to keep life going.

The moment the sun rises they are excited to improvise a new dialogue with nature, to treat it well, to feel the impact of mutual respect, to obtain the abundant fruits of this dedication. The exuberance of their life becomes very present in every work. Whether someone is a farmer, a fisherman, a carpenter, a constructor, a musician, an artist, a basket designer, a fortuneteller, a spiritual doctor, a magician, old or young, man or woman – everyone is there ready to let life happen.

Life in the village was carefree. I felt so much joy to roam through the bushes with no restrictions. I embraced the freedom of not being restricted, as I was in my parent's home. Kids in the village had few rules and were taught how to be independent at a very young age. If they were around their parents, most of the time it was the mother. They went hunting, farmed, and did other manly stuff with their dads, but affection was mostly from their mothers.

We followed our cousins to go hunting with dogs. We killed a raccoon, groundhogs, and other bush animals. These days I regret having hunted animals, but at the time I was just a child exploring a new world of adventures in the wild, feeling a fundamental sense of manhood begin to unfold in me so easily and fast.

My cousin MP, whom we knew better than our other cousins, introduced me to making traps for the groundhogs, catfish, and other wildlife. He would stutter but was very talkative and enjoyed recognition. He taught me how to swim in a river, cook and eat goat's blood, eat with my hands, and travel through the bushes to nearby villages on foot. Everything was so savage and powerful.

When we wanted to swim, we had to announce our arrival at the creek. The road leading to the river was very narrow, so nobody was able to see far left, right, backward or forward. The curves were avoiding big trees, big rocks, and hills, among other things. We needed to announce ourselves approximately 50 feet before we approached the river in order to respect those who might be bathing there. Everybody bathed there, so if the opposite sex was using the river, one had to wait.

The Kissi, like many of the other native groups, believe that the spirits of their ancestors act as mediators between them and God. They trust that a supernatural world interacts with their life whether they want it to or not. Good and evil spirits can quickly turn into living creatures or objects. Someone can fall severely ill, and even die, as a consequence of evil practices performed everywhere around. Therefore, the need for spiritual practices conducted by a gifted shaman is required to receive immediate protection.

Sometimes a spiritual guide, dotted with supernatural powers, is consulted as a private spiritual Investigator to find out if the cause of a death or one's suffering of a terrible illness had been provoked by someone who had sent an evil force with the intention to harm a particular person or a family.

Even though some people of the Kissi communities fear evil rituals, they have been doing these practices for generations. Perhaps because they believe that those darkest forces from the occult have the power of damaging their life at any time, they choose to seek refuge in Christianity. I know my family has done so. They have known very well that it is best not to arouse nor provoke the energies of darkness – nobody can control them once they are released. It is preferable to keep them away from our thoughts and surrender our lives to a Christian God, compassionate and pure, who would never use his supreme force to harm anyone – not even nature.

Their spiritual traditions include a belief in a supreme God as well as in the spirits of nature and the veneration of ancestors. They keep the doors open between the human and the spiritual world to harmonize nature with the supernatural.

During religious practices they usually create divinatory rites to achieve a hypnotic trance stimulated by the constant beat of a drumming session and singing. Their purpose is to "receive" a transcendent spirit, which will manifest itself through their bodies to express a particular message, to heal a person or a situation, and, in some cases, to harm someone who has become an enemy.

Aside from worshiping all kinds of spirits, they pray to their predecessors for them to intermediate between themselves and the Supreme Creator God.

It is believed that deities, spirits, and the dead need to be honored. During their ritual ceremonies they pour a precious liquid or rice, sometimes offering rice into running water. Rituals can include the sacrifice of animals, flowers, cooked food, and crops – among other gifts.

They embrace the natural phenomena as an open book of wisdom to receive divine guidance and even to provide healing of all kinds. Sorcerers and diviners are consulted on a regular basis. Sometimes the spirits are represented by small stone statues that are worshiped and offered during animal sacrifices by the chief of the village. Praying to deceased relatives to gain their help from the other world is a regular practice.

As my parents and grandparents have converted to Christianity, they never wanted for us to explore any animistic religious practices, not even to wonder, only to pray and behave.

Even though Grandma and Grandpa from my father's side were both Christians, Granddaddy had a charm that he believed would bring him good luck. During the days and weeks he used his magic tool, he didn't eat any food with salt. The belief was that salt would weaken the power of the amulet. Therefore, Grandma cooked for him without salt.

Grandpa's charm would bring him luck, good health, protection against enemies, and strength. Nobody else needed to have an amulet because if he were under its powers, every member of his family and descendants would be lucky too.

I learned that the people from a nearby village about a 15-20 minute walk from my dad's village worship a group of catfish living in a creek on the outskirts of the village. I wanted to explore these spiritual practices because I was wondering if it would be possible that God could communicate to us through the messages of these fish. A friend of our family took me there, and we walked early in the morning to avoid the extreme heat of the season. What I saw was magnificent. They pound the rice into rice-dust to feed the fish with rice.

Even though the communities eat catfish, no one is allowed to catch and eat the catfish from this creek. To the village people these are not ordinary catfish. They are a source of spiritual blessings. There is a belief that the fish in this river have the power to bring them a good harvest of their crops, a blessing for healthy children, and protection for the village.

To observe the cycles of nature and to flow with them – it was something that I have learned from the Kisses through my parents. They were accustomed to teaching unselfish behaviors to support other people's needs. They developed their life through selfless cooperation. Probably thousands of years of connection with farming have cultivated in them a respectful attitude toward people as well as toward nature.

Once a woman gives birth, the whole village comes with a gift, which could be cattle, fish, crops from their gardens and farms, or clothes. Women would support the mother while helping her with the child or her other kids if she needed an extra hand. If someone died, everybody in the village would come together and help the bereaved family with funeral arrangements, burial, and contribute financially to help the family even after the burial.

They did the same with farming. They organized groups to help each other with different aspects of the agricultural process. Men would hold groups to fell the trees and clear the forest. During those days the women would be responsible for the cooking. When it came time to plant the crops, mainly rice, the men, women, and older kids would work together. Women organized themselves into groups to pick the weeds from among the rice. They used mostly their bare hands and small digging holes to get all the weeds out from among the rice. Farms would usually range from a few lots to a few acres. The thicker the forest was before planting, the fewer weeds they were likely to get.

While the women worked on the weeds, the men would build a fence around the crops, mostly rice, to prevent animals – especially groundhogs – from eating the plants or damaging them. If it was a rice farm, then the older kids, both boys and girls – but mostly boys – would be responsible for keeping the birds from eating the rice.

During harvest, groups of men, women, and children use little curvy knives to harvest the rice. It is done during the dry season. These are fun times when families have a surplus of food and some money from their crops to purchase clothes and other things they need. Christmas and the new year are the biggest celebrations in all of the country, from small villages to large cities.

Most of the art consists of objects of a utilitarian purpose such as baskets and vertical looms. However, they have unusual carved stone statues called "Pombo," which means "the deceased." They worship this soapstone with anthropomorphic carvings. They are made for ritual ceremonies with the purpose of receiving protection from predators. They believed that the figures carried supernatural powers.

During the festivities they would wrap the statues with cotton and pour sacrificial blood on them. Later, the statue would be placed on the owner's family altar to receive protection against any disease. They also would set them over small shrines built on the rice field to receive the blessings of an abundant harvest. These ritual figures had been passed down through generations for as long as 800 years. They spread these ceremonial figures in fields, rivers, rice fields, and family altars. Still today the Kissi people keep up the tradition of stone carving. Some of these carvings were the abodes of the spirits of their ancestors. They used to consult a diviner to find out which spiritual ancestor lived in a statue.

Music for them does not need a melody to nurture their spirit. The rhythmic sound of drumming and whistling, together with the vocal cords that I have found only in African DNA, can unleash earth energies. The force of their voices can be compared to the fierce thunderstorms during the rainy seasons.

The stories I've received from the mysterious culture of my ancestors portray a very rich imagination, which is constantly nourished by a mythology as exuberant as it is enigmatic.

I heard once about a neighbor who, in spite of converting to Christianity, became very active in the practice of tribal religion. He performed all kinds of weird movements and chants when he would host spirits from the other world. These spirits would enter into his body to provide him with a special guidance during the healing acts he performed on a person, circumstance, or animal that needed to be healed. He was a witch doctor, a greegree-man, a shaman. People went to see him to receive the cures for all those things they considered to be spiritual sicknesses. I don't remember his name, but he was quite popular in the village. People visited him in his humble hut and paid him with rice or small animals that they could carry in hand. He would cure diseases with a black magic formula; he would promote through his magic spells that people would receive their stolen things – even a stolen soul that had been offered to the evil spirits.

Aside from the spiritual powers attributed to the catfish, there was a tree that possessed something even more fascinating. It was not just any tree; it involved different aspects of spirituality where forces of the light and darkness were invited to unfold their religious practices at its foot. It was called the cotton tree, and it outlined a majestic presence in the landscape of the villages. For years many Liberian villages venerated the cotton tree with the belief that it would ward off malignant spirits and keep away evil forces.

The Kissi people from the village of my ancestors worshiped a tree bigger than I'd ever seen before. Even though the cotton tree grows in all kinds of tropical climates, the one from Liberia is one of the biggest varieties. It holds all kinds of sacred meanings to some Liberians. It has such a mystical power that whenever someone would suggest cutting the tree to prevent branches from falling and hurting nearby homes, crops, or even people, a significant resistance prevented its removal. And it was very likely that despite all the damage that could occur, the tree would remain there. Parents always warned their children to stay away from these cotton trees.

Even though the elders in the family didn't want us to go near a cotton tree, I needed to see its wonders with my own eyes. It was hard to believe that a tree would be able to harm a person or provide some sort of magical powers, so I secretly went there with one of my cousins.

The biggest cotton tree in Hundoni was known for being the dwelling place of witchcraft activities. The Kissi communities revered it, and the sorcerers offered it their ancient witchcraft. It is believed that witches used brooms to fly in and out of this big cotton tree at night.

What I saw was a magnificent organic sculpture spreading all along its immense roots and mysterious folds. I was amazed by its fruits coming out of the branches as a cotton fiber. Its height sustained with royal elegance its head and shoulders above the rest of the trees. I could see how a powerful myth had been created from its presence. The fiber of the cotton fruit resembled a macabre mask, as if an unfortunate spirit had been trapped during a night of fiendish rituals.

Since its trunk was covered by deep folds, similar to thick curtains of wood, anyone could hide between its gaps and vanish from view. I wanted to enter into its layers, but my cousin warned me not to do it. Someone could disappear in there forever. It is believed that the trunk possesses dimensional doors through which sorcerers are allowed to visit other worlds. They could also make someone die, swallowed by the evil forces that might be hidden in there.

Some people said that it attacks the intruders and benefits those who worship him – like the warlocks. Others believed that the sharp thorns of the trunk were the clutches of a demon that could dig into the skin to absorb the blood of those who dared to climb. The people of the villages have learned to respect him and fear him.

For a moment it seemed to me that the branches were moving as if a strong wind were shaking them. But there was no wind. Perhaps we had succumbed to the power of suggestion. Perhaps we imagined everything. But we didn't stay to find out and ran toward the village without looking back.

As we were approaching our homes, we passed in front of the house of the most revered sorcerer of the village. He was burning some sacred aromatic leaves on charcoal. He didn't look at us, but he was laughing. We kept going. My cousin walked tensely. He was pale. I vividly remember the smell of those leaves floating through a very thick smoke. It made me feel as if I were on the journey of a spiritual ceremony.

Life there was very different from the one we used to know. There were lots of mosquitos, no electricity, and no running water. But we lived there surrounded by myths, magic, and wondrous adventures. By the grace of God we were fine and enjoyed the family time living in the village of our ancestors. We stayed there, protected in our tribal shelter until the rebels came closer and took over Foya, Hundonin, and the rest of the villages in the Foya district.

Those were dreadful times. People were killed, women and girls were raped, and men were taken to jail for various reasons. Some were forced to join the rebels, especially the children, and others were made to work for the rebels in different capacities. It was tough and fearful, especially without the protection of our father.

Our mother had to do everything she could to protect us and provide for us. As God would have it, our uncles, especially my uncle Miller, had made available the space we lived in. He made sure that we had food to eat every day. It was a good time to be with those family members, especially to have the time to spend with our grandmother – my father's mother – but unfortunately, my grandfather had died long before the civil war, so I never had the opportunity to see him. But we had this time to learn about him and feel very close to him because he was from Hundonin, and we were able to see where he lived and where he was buried, along with our other uncles, cousins, and various relatives. But under the conditions that the rebels had created, it was very scary to be walking around. We witnessed a lot of gun firing, people being treated badly by the rebels, people being beaten severely, wounded on various parts of their bodies. We saw how rebels were looting people's homes, forcing young and old people to carry these looted goods to different places in Foya.

Meanwhile, more and more displaced people, from other parts of the country that were previously captured by the rebels, continued their walk towards Foya. Some were able to cross the border to Guinea and some remained in Foya.

I remember two brothers who had walked for more than a week, day and night through the bushes, under different weather conditions, from Monrovia, the capital of Liberia, to where I was in the village of my ancestors, Hundonin. They were heading to Foya and later to Sierra Leone. I was happy to see these courageous young men dare to risk a dangerous encounter with the rebels to gain freedom outside of Liberia – to keep growing in a promising land. I heard them talking when my mother gave them food and water. It was the first time they had eaten in weeks. They were pursuing the life they could no longer have in our country. They sat down, ate, drank, rested, and they were so grateful. We became friends from the first time we met. These brothers wanted to study at the university in Sierra Leone, or wherever life might take them. After a while they decided to continue their journey to Foya, which was about one hour walking from the village of Hundonin where we stayed. They took their belongings, placed them on their heads, and began to walk. They promised that they would return and spend more time with us. Little did we know what was ahead of them.

Once in Foya, they were arrested because one of them was very tall. He was well built and during those times, people of such a strong stature were often considered by the rebels to be ex-soldiers of the sitting government. So, needless to say, he was charged with being a soldier of the government. He was poorly treated, beaten badly, and tied up with both hands behind his back. He was severely beaten with ropes, knives, and guns, among other weapons the rebels would use to harm people. Then he was locked up in jail. Days later they were released from jail and placed in a house where the rebels kept prisoners. They remained there for weeks. One day, on a Saturday, some friends and I went to the Foya market; Saturdays were very popular for shopping because people from the neighboring villages would come to the marketplace in Foya and bring their various goods to sell.

Saturdays in Foya became blessed days. It was on that Saturday that I saw one of the brothers again. He told me that they had not come back to the village to see us due to the bad treatment they had received from the rebels. He was even afraid to leave Foya to go anywhere. They had been forced to join the rebels. One of the brothers had to go and fight. Unfortunately, with the limited training he had, he'd been killed.

Later on I heard that the other had made his way across the border to Sierra Leone. There are hundreds of stories from the thousands of people that walked for months to Foya, to Sierra Leone, to the Ivory Coast, to Guinea, and to the other parts of the country.

Our father came to take us back to our devastated town Voinjama.

With the bitter feeling that it might be the last time I would be with the family of my ancestors, a sentimental act of melancholy made me run up to embrace my grandmother and my uncle Fayia Miller. He allowed me to touch his amulet and told me with a confident smile, "Everything will be fine – you are with us and we are with you wherever you go. Nobody will ever be able to *steal* the power that lives in your beautiful soul. You are departing now, but you will always be in our hearts." He kissed me and kindly pushed me toward my father.

I left the village with the hope that when I grow up I will visit my family back in the village as often as I can. Little did I know, I was going away for more than a decade if not decades.

Chapter Six

FLEEING AGAIN

MY FATHER CAME to the village of our ancestors in Foya to take us back to Voinjama when things there had become very dangerous. Meanwhile, Voinjama seemed to become a safer place to return home to. My mother couldn't follow us this time. She needed to stay in Foya with my sister Teta to finish some business.

Once again we were fleeing, and I was sad. I was leaving behind experiences that I knew I would no longer be able to enjoy. And although I didn't want it to happen, a vital part of my childhood began to vanish the farther we moved away from the land of my ancestors.

Early that morning we walked from the village of my grandparents toward Foya to board upon the back of a semi-truck that would take us to Voinjama. I knew I would miss that mystical time with Grandmother and uncles: their traditions, their beliefs, and their powerful way of unfolding magic where there was nothing.

The road was dangerous to drive on with so many pot-holes. In some places it was appalling, muddy and slippery. We had to walk down to a certain spot and wait for the truck driver to come. His workers had to use shovels to move some of the mud in the way of the truck's tires to avoid slipping. They also laid down planks for the truck's tires to roll over to avoid getting stuck in the mud.

After several hours of driving over that damaged road, we arrived at our home in Voinjama. A different Voinjama. All of the businesses had been looted. Buildings and houses were abandoned. Some of my close friends were now rebels. All of our cattle and farm animals – pigs, chickens, and ducks – were gone. The rebels had wiped out everything that we had, except our willingness to start all over again and again.

Life had turned into a territory of unimaginable dangers for the simple minds of the people of Voinjama. We had rebels living among us. They were "killing machines," proud of being murderers. We saw young men walking around with guns all day long. Very often we heard gunfire. People were living in fear. I learned to live in fear too.

The marketplace that used to be very crowded on Fridays had become a landscape of depressing shapes, colors and faces. Everything had become a living death territory since the early months when the rebels took over Voinjama. Six months after their attack, our town's pulse was slowing as if it were in a deathlike coma. All of the schools were still closed. Government offices had been looted and shut down. There was no running water. No electricity. We used a lantern to provide us with light and kerosene to power it.

In spite of the sadness that was breathed in Voinjama, we managed to stay a long time before being forced to flee again.

My father, two of my elder sisters (Rose and Onike) with their sons (Ivan and Joe) had to stay back to make all the necessary arrangements before they could join us later. I left with Jestina, Saah, Fayiah, Fallah, and Sia under the custody of our uncle Obeto. My dad, my sister Onike, her son Puchew, and Rose and her son Ivan stayed in Voinjama for a little while before they departed too.

Our plan was to flee to Foya to meet our mother and sister (Teta) before leaving Liberia if possible. This time we did not have a car to take us to Foya. We walked through the bushes accompanied by our uncle for protection. We walked all night and the journey was scary and full of dangers. It was a rough trip. All the roads were dark – the only light we had was the moonlight. Sometimes we had to wade through water up to our knees. For some of us children it reached our waists. We had to walk through this black water that we couldn't see through and that was not safe at all. There could be stumps or rocks. Snakes. Anything. But we cautiously walked through, by the grace of God. We climbed hills that I didn't think I could climb. The long way to freedom took us through valleys, people's farms, and lots of thick and complicated bushes, without any tools to help us to pass safely. I remember one point when we were climbing a hill along the border of Guinea and Liberia overlooking the Makona River that separates Liberia from Guinea. We walked all along the Makona River on the Liberian side, seeing Guinea across through a bunch of bushes.

Everything was very vivid and scary. We were crossing the side of the river infected by the militia while on the Guinea side everything seemed to be peaceful. There were no rebels there. No Civil War. No horror. We heard a lot of gunshots and sounds of other atrocities: the screaming and mourning from the echoes of the wind. They could be close or they could be far. We kept on going, focusing our minds on reaching a safe land of freedom and life.

We looked across the river, but we couldn't easily be in a protected territory due to the river being in the way of the land. So, we walked from the shore of the Makona River along the bushes to Foya. We saw a large group of people again. There were hundreds. We were walking through different villages. Sometimes the road was very narrow, and we had to take the path through bushes where there was water up to knee level. Some little children had to be carried. We didn't know what was in the water as we walked through it. It was very frightening to think that we might be stepping right into danger. We just had to walk through that water while carrying all of our belongings the best that we could. I had my school backpack with a few books in it. Others had suitcases, bags, dishes, food, blankets, and mattresses. We walked in darkness through the water and the bushes.

We walked all night until we arrived at a small town. To my surprise I saw our neighbors, friends from school with their parents; as children we were excited to see each other, and some kids were even playing while the older people were busy worrying about what was happening. But we were not able to stay long, my uncle told us with concern in his voice.

We had to keep walking, and we left again that night. We headed to a town about two hours away.

It was still dark when we arrived at Toumogizo. Most of our friends were about to cross the Makona River – the border between Liberia and Guinea. As terrible as it sounds, the children and elders, the sick and the healthy– all of us – were fleeing from horrendous deaths.

In those gloomy hours our eyes had been shadowed by the torment of what had been lived– or what we had lost. The grief and fear accompanied us wherever we went. It was difficult to trust. The enemy could easily infiltrate within the innocence of young friends to provoke a massive attack and a massacre – like what had happened in the places we were fleeing from. It was a silent night. The air was thick and the wind remained still like a pause in eternity. I could hear canoes entering softly into the waters of the Makona River. It seemed as if for a moment life had dared to flow once more toward a shore that promised us the hope of a new start. The little children clung to their mothers' arms – probably the safest place around. They might have thought that they were going to play somewhere else, but there was no fun waiting for any of us wherever we were going. And we had to keep moving, in spite of the dangerous circumstances that surrounded us.

Most of the people that walked with us that night were crossing the river to Guinea, but my uncle Obeto decided we were going to continue walking toward Foya. My whole body was aching. For days, we had walked through bushes, and sometimes on the main road, which was not paved. They were dusty roads with a lot of potholes everywhere. We walked up hills, down valleys, along rivers, through more bushes, and across little roads for days. There were endless trails that we walked with my little brother, Fallah, who fortunately didn't suffer from any of his frequent seizures. We had to flee in such a rush that we were not able to prepare what we needed for our long journey. We had no food, no water, and no medicine for Fallah. The only water we found along the way to drink was from dirty and contaminated creeks.

Only when we passed through a village did my uncle find us food and clean water. After walking for more than three days, we arrived at Foya– but this time we couldn't visit the village of my grandparents.

We stayed in my uncle's home in Foya for a little while before crossing to Guinea. It was in his house that our little Fallah began having his epileptic seizures again. Fortunately, my mother was able to get his medicine from a pharmacy in town.

But something was wrong in Foya. It was still under the command of the Charles Taylor militia led by the so-called General Fayia. The atmosphere was very scary and risky, and civilians avoided the streets that were populated with militia loyal to General Fayia.

Their mission was to arrest, detain, and kill a group of their fellow rebels fleeing with us from Voinjama to Foya. The fleeing rebels belonged mostly to the Mano and Gio tribes of Nimba County. Among those were a Kissi colonel, Jacob

Gbankefay, and his group. General Fayia and his men accused the fleeing rebels of selling Voinjama to ULIMO (United Liberation Movement of Liberia for Democracy), a rebel group that was founded in May 1991. This consisted mostly of Krahn soldiers seeking refuge in Sierra Leone. They had fought in the Armed Forces of Liberia (AFL). Many members of the Mandingo tribe were slaughtered by Taylor's militia. ULIMO was initially led by Raleigh Seekie, a deputy minister of finance during the late President Samuel Doe's government. ULIMO forces penetrated western Liberia in September 1991 and gained significant areas held by Charles Taylor's NPFL. These areas were the diamond mining areas of Lofa and Bomi counties. Needless to say, these were crucial areas for Charles Taylor to obtain.

In 1994 due to internal divisions, ULIMO broke into two separate militias: ULIMO-J, a Krahn-based faction led by General Roosevelt Johnson and ULIMO-K, a Mandingo based faction led by Alhaji G.V. Kromah.

The Lofians, with the exception of the Mandingos, took no chances with ULIMO. The majority of the Lofians, belonging primarily to the Lorma, Gbandi, and Kissi ethnic groups, will argue that the atrocity and looting imposed on them by ULIMO was by far worse than that of Charles Taylor and his NPFL.

Once in Foya, General Fayia and his men launched explosives, followed by continuous heavy shooting at night. The rumors were secretly circulating the next morning. They have been attacked, but given the vigilance and voodoo that General Fayia had acquired from witch doctors, he was able to single-handedly run off the enemies, killing the majority of them. The entire Foya (notoriously Foya Air Field), was in a state of panic. The atmosphere seemed cloudy.

But voodoo magic didn't last long. Eventually, a real attack on General Fayia and his men was destined to happen. The Mano and Gio fighters came through the bushes as ferocious animals after their prey. Finally, they attacked General Fayia and his men, forcing them to flee into the surrounding villages. It was during this period of absence of General Fayia and his men that the attackers set free those whom Fayia had in prison at the former palm mill in Chaysenin. Among those released was Colonel Gbankefay and some of his men. Gbankefay accidentally ran across me and my siblings at my uncle's house. According to him, he thought we had been captured and killed by General Fayia.

Thank God for the wisdom and courage of my older brother Saah, who insisted we had to leave the large group with which we had been travelling during our over three days' walking from Voinjama to Foya with our uncle Obeto. I remember that we reluctantly agreed with him and took off. It was here in Bandaini where we left Gbankefay and other big-name rebels and their soldiers to continue our walk toward Foya.

Our only consolation during these terrifying times began when we found an abandoned sweet puppy. She was brown and about the size of a Yorkie. She consistently followed us everywhere like a Guardian Angel. She was named Renin by my cousin Mike. Renin was able to make me laugh in spite of all the horror around us. I believed she had adopted us. She knew how to make me understand anytime she got tired of walking. I took her and carried her in my arms.

Gbankefay told us just before we left that those militiamen loyal to General Fayia had attacked and arrested all the rebels who traveled with us from Voinjama. They were stripped naked, two elbows pulled behind their backs, tied and thrown into the back of pickup trucks and taken to the old palm mill somewhere outside Foya in Chaysenin. General Fayia and others beat them with guns, knives and sticks before locking them up in a container. They described the place as dark and horrible. He said that most of them had been killed by Fayia and his men. That's why he thought that Fayia and his men might have arrested us along the way. This could have been true. But by the grace and mercy of God, they went right past us while we were hiding behind the house at a checkpoint.

After we left Gbankefay and others in a town called Bandaini, we also left our Uncle Obeto and family in Shelloe, a village close to Foya. Being away from our parents was very unusual; being away with other people and rebels in unknown places under harsh conditions with our precious Fallah was extreme.

We arrived at Shelloe, the village of the most respected Paramount Chief in all of the Kissi Chiefdom, if not all of Lofa county, Chief Tamba Taylor. Uncle Obeto made a stop at Chief Tamba Taylor's house in Shelloe and began an unending conversation. We quickly inquired from the villagers how far Foya was, and we found that we were pretty close to entering it. We ran to ask uncle Obeto permission to continue to Foya by ourselves to see our mother.

On our way toward Foya was a checkpoint. They stopped and interrogated us. Even though we feared the worst, we were trained to keep calm and pretend that we were locals coming from the nearest village behind us we could remember. From our appearance and the way we spoke, they knew we were not from the area. We had no money and not much on us to carry except a backpack and Renin, our puppy. They let us go but took our puppy. Saah, who always insisted that we keep moving ahead, didn't want to leave her. She had become a beloved member of our family. At that moment we heard a sound of a car coming from afar, and the soldiers at the checkpoint got attentive and ordered us to run behind the building and hide. We managed to sneak there in time. Two pickup trucks full of soldiers stopped briefly at the checkpoint. We overheard them asking if they have seen anybody from Voinjama. After they denied that, the person that I assumed was General Fayia himself ordered them to detain anyone coming through the checkpoint from Voinjama. The group hurried back into their pickups and pulled out.

One of the soldiers at the checkpoint came and told us to leave immediately. He advised that if General Fayiah found us, he would kill us. I was on my toes to take off when Saah continued to plead for the dog, stating that we couldn't leave without our puppy. Even Jestina, who was the oldest sibling among us, told him to forget the dog and let's go, but he insisted. With no time to continuing arguing, the soldier gave us our puppy back.

We were just about to leave when a boy approached us and introduced himself as Kebbie. He was very nice and friendly. He knew us and our dad from Voinjama. He even knew our Uncle Pawa and our cousins very well. I am not sure where Kebbie was going and we did not ask, but he volunteered to take us through a back road and straight to our Uncle Pawa's house to avoid any more checkpoints and danger on the way. I believed that God had sent him to save us. Without him, we wouldn't have been able to make it to Foya.

The name General Fayia was strange and we did not understand how serious it was, and neither were we interested in knowing anything about the name or the person. Kebbie took us through the back roads all the way to our uncle's house.

Gbankefay advised us to leave Foya on that accidental encounter, saying that it was risky for us. But he also encouraged us to flee as soon as we could. As General Fayia took control of Foya, the fight between him and the Mano and Gio continued. That's when our mother decided to take us across the border to Guinea in small numbers until we were all able to cross. We got on a semi-truck with the marketers and their products. We left Foya with the intention to cross the border to Guinea. On board the truck was my mother, my sister Teta, Fayia, Fallah, my niece Sia and I.

Unfortunately for us, when we got to the border that night, it was closed. There was no canoe in the water to take us across. They had emptied the truck of all the bags of coffee, cocoa, drums of oil and other containers of oranges. People were making their way into town to find a place to sleep until the next morning. I sat down on a coffee bag, exhausted and with an injured foot from all the walking the previous weeks. I was trying to think about what might be waiting for us next when I saw a rebel walking determinedly towards me – perhaps because I looked visibly different. It was my first time in this part of the country.

He stood in front of me with an arrogant attitude and asked for my name.

"I am Tamba," I said.

"What's your last name?" he asked in an aggressive tone

"Porter, My name is Tamba," I replied.

He made an expression as if he had just heard something bad. And that bad thing was my last name, Porter. I did not then know, nor did any of my siblings or my mother knew, that the rebels had listed my dad as one of the people that supported ULIMO. Our father had been accused of collaborating with the ULIMO group that was fighting against the crimes of Taylor's forces. They had a list of people who had been connected with the ULIMO militia. They were hunting ULIMO supporters and followers to execute them in their horrifying way of killing their prisoners. My dad was on their list. We did not know anything about it.

When I said that my name was Tamba, I pronounced my death sentence. He remembered the Porter they were looking for. He asked me to stay there and went to talk to his commander. He told him that he had just run across a Porter. I was terrified. The leader and some of the other rebels walked toward me.

"Are you Mr. Porter's son?" he asked with disgust in his voice.

"Yes, I am," I responded.

"Who did you come here with?" he shouted.

"With my mom and my siblings," I said.

He called my mother and requested that my little brother show up too. He told my mom that he was going to arrest my brother and me and take us to jail. We knew that meant death. My mother would not be able to change that, and she needed to protect my sister from the possibility of being raped and killed as well.

Immediately, he ordered his soldiers and rebels to take us to what they called his G2 office. And he told my mom that he wasn't going to arrest her because she was someone else's child, but that my brother and I were children of Mr. Porter and for that reason we were under arrest. Even though my sister Teta was also a Porter, they didn't want her. I assumed it was because she spoke in the Kissi language to them; therefore, she didn't belong to those ethnic groups considered the enemies. So, it never occurred to them that she could have been a Porter. Whatever the case, she was not on death row as my brother and I were.

The commander at this G2 office was Mr. Budoo. When he saw us, he ordered his soldiers to take us to his office and to step outside. They planned to lock us up that night and execute us the next night, or lead us back to Foya until our execution.

That was a terrifying moment for my brother and me. Commander Budoo made us understand that we were in terrible danger – that our father had been accused of supporting ULIMO, and we could face the same torture and be killed after suffering a long agony. He walked impatiently along his office looking at the floor and wiggling his head. I did not know whether he was going to kill us there with his own hands or punish us with the whip on his desk. Then he stopped. He looked at me and I held my little brother's hand. He approached us with a severe gesture and told us that he had decided not to lock us up. He wanted to release us because he had deep gratitude to my father. Before the Civil War began, he wanted to attend a school in Voinjama, but he didn't have the resources to support his education nor a place to stay, until he met my father.

At that time my dad was a professor at the school and he felt touched by the desire of this young boy wanting to develop a better life through his studies. My dad had not only taken care of this commander when he was a child, but he had also fully supported his education until he received his high school diploma. I couldn't believe what I was hearing! Not only was this commander willing to release my brother and me from a terrible death, but my father had also became a humanitarian hero.

In spite of his decision of releasing us that night, the commander was in an awkward situation. The least he could do was to let us leave the G2 office and find a place to go. He had someone contact our mother to come to the G2 office and they, together with some other people, figured out a way to take us to a nearby village called Solomba.

Around 10 at night we arrived at a house of some friends of my mother who soon received us in Solomba. When we were about to eat, a group of rebels surrounded the house and some of them came to the door and forced it open. The one who had a weapon called an RPG was standing at the door. The others had AK47s and other arms to show their ferocious power. The leader of the group walked inside and looked around. I had a piece of bread in my hands. I believed I was frozen. He approached closer and closer, and then he shook his head saying:

"OK. I just wanted to be sure that you won't go anywhere!" After he said that, he left, screaming like an animal. My sister said there was not any time to lose, and she ran to someone she knew that worked on a truck, a semi-truck. His name was Prince. She asked him to take my brother and me to a place far from the deadly clutches of the rebels. The next morning my mom and sister made all the arrangements for us to get back on board the back of the truck to Foya because where we were staying we would have been killed.

We had to walk from Solomba toward the river, where the truck was waiting for us. The truck had a trailer full of goods. There were people in the trailer. My mother encouraged my little brother Fayia and me to jump into it. And we did. But the commander who had requested our arrest at the border was in the front seat of the pickup truck. He saw us getting into the trailer. He opened the door, jumped out of the truck, grabbed my little brother and pulled him off the truck. He nearly fell. My mother broke down and started crying. We were all very nervous. Then the commander got back into the truck and it took off.

Even though I was relieved because we were not in jail, I was confused about his reaction. He knew we had to be in prison, but he left us there and drove away –maybe because there was no place for us to escape to in the bush of this tiny village. We wouldn't know how to get away. He knew that we were in an environment that we wouldn't be able to leave. The only means of transportation out of that village was the pickup truck he was driving and the semi-truck that had brought us to the border. He had total control of both means of transportation.

Between Guinea and us was a river. But there was no canoe available. The border was temporarily closed for several days. My mom and sister talked to Prince, to the owner of the truck, and to some other people she knew, asking them to protect us. They all promised her they would hide us. She put us on board the truck when it was about to leave and took us back to Foya.

We did not cross the border to Guinea that first attempt, and we didn't know then how long we would have to stay until we would be able to cross the border toward Guinea and begin there our life as refugees.

Chapter Seven

THE DANGER WE SURVIVED

STILL TODAY I wonder what were the causes of all the atrocities we all experienced in our country during the years of the "Civil War." What was the unstoppable force that unleashed a tremendous amount of hatred and the desire to annihilate our roots, our hopes, and the future generations who were not able to find refuge in a compassionate shelter, as we had been blessed to receive?

There were so many other horrific events during those years of the Liberian Civil War. The atmosphere leading up to the first attack was very tense. The rebels were coming, and nobody knew when. Some Liberians could not believe the rebels would ever severely harm civilians, and their bloody attack took our country by surprise.

My Friend Jallah used to live on 24th street close to the John F. Kennedy Memorial Hospital in Sinkor Monrovia. He told me how civilians avoided the streets and remained in their houses, fearing for their lives. Members of the AFL (Armed Forces of Liberia) patrolled the streets with heavy guns and were well-prepared for war. They broke into homes of civilians in their so-called search for rebels. During this process, they killed innocent civilians.

Jallah lived with his family in a gated compound that had a watchman to guard the gate. He was a civilian with no gun. One day they saw from inside the house how members of the AFL were dragging the guard from the window. With sadness and fear, my friend saw how this young man was screaming for his life. After those soldiers had unmercifully beaten the man with their guns, he received multiple shots and was dragged, dead, to the driveway of my friend Jallah's house. Screaming ferociously, they forced my friend to open his door and demanded everybody out, asking if there was any rebel living in the house. Those were moments of endless terror. When he and his family denied having a rebel hidden in their house, the soldiers counted seven members of the family and warned them that if the next day there was an extra person, everybody would be exterminated. The same would occur if they found fewer than seven people.

The soldiers instructed them to get rid of everything that was red in the house because it was the color of the rebels. They ordered them to remove the dead body from the driveway. Wrapped in deep sadness, they brought the remains of the poor guard and buried the body in a shallow hole not too far from the house.

Just when they were about to return to the house, they saw the same group of soldiers stop a lady walking across the street. She was wearing a colorful dress with flowers on it which were predominantly red; they severely beat her, shot her, dragged her dead body to the same driveway and commanded Jallah and his family to bury her.

A few days later they heard a group of people crying for their lives in a white pickup truck that drove by with soldiers torturing the victims. They turned toward the beach. After they heard a series of gunshots, they saw the pickup truck returning with no civilians.

My friend's mother decided they had to move across the bridge to Logan Town. On their way to that place, they were stopped after the bridge by members of the Prince Johnson INPFL, which controlled that part of Monrovia. During the interrogation, one of the rebels pulled out his gun and pointed between Jallah and a lady and shot a man slightly behind them. Then the soldier took a step toward the dead body and shot him again, and again, shouting that he was one of those who used to enjoy money from the government.

Any man whose presence looked healthy and educated became enough reason to conclude that he worked or used to work for the government. And this was a death sentence.

With a crazy tension in his face, the soldier approached my friend and took him out of the group, threatening that he was going to kill him. Jallah's mom began to cry and plead for her son. Fortunately for him, a higher ranking rebel pulled up in a pickup truck and commanded all the soldiers to jump onboard. He left Jallah and hopped in the pickup truck, and that's how Jallah life was saved. He and the rest of the people continued their journey across the bridge to Logan Town.

The civil war left the country brutalized, its people traumatized, and its economy in pieces. It unleashed egregious violations of human rights as the fighting forces engaged in horrendous brutality toward combatants and civilians. Their tactics were designed to terrorize the population, and they developed the domain of evil. In some places, they forced displacement to clear the area for their occupation. Many farmers were ordered to abandon their lands, leaving the crops on the ground and parts of the fields unplanted.

All the massacres that took place in churches, schools, and many public, and private places compelled many Liberians to flee the country. Families became separated, and displaced as civilians were taken away or fled.

A survivor from Camp Schieffelin told us that on his way to find a secure refuge, he saw a man begging for his life on his knees. Without any compassion, rebels opened fire on him. The survivor managed to hide and heard them screaming, "We want to see blood," and they ran to their truck to pull out more people they kept there to continue their killings.

The extreme grade of violence that occurred in many places was not isolated, but it was a strategy to encourage brutal methods or even actions by the faction leaders themselves "to teach" how to unfold the worst level of cruelty anyone could ever imagine. Civilians became the collateral damage and intended target of the enemy forces, Taylor's NPLF and those that came to resist them.

It is very painful and hard to describe the atrocities committed by both rebels and government soldiers, but releasing them from my memories and the memories of those innocent people perhaps would help us to heal this past and to prevent this inhumane behavior from happening again.

The rebels were looking for Doe's followers, workers, and for his native ethnicity, the Krahn tribe – besides the massive and horrific killings of the Mandingos and other indigenous groups. They began going house-to-house as desperation began arousing a kind of dread that nobody had experienced before.

In another tragedy, the Duport Road Cow Field Massacre in December 1994, more than 44 people were massacred, allegedly by forces of the NPFL. Among those killed was a pregnant woman whose stomach was split open with a knife, her head cut off, her baby killed in her belly, and then both were burned. The rebels poured gasoline on the home and burned it down with them still inside. The pregnant woman's legs and arms were burned to ashes. The remainder of her body was left with the burned baby still in her stomach. My cousins, who lived close to Duport Road, heard the crying and were afraid for their lives and dared not to come out. The only thing that spared their lives was the checkpoint of EOCMOG (The Economic Community of West African States Monitoring Group) that was close to where they live. That night, even ECOMOG was unable to save the victims. It was a night of brutal killings with knives and other weapons. The rebels burned a house while the whole family was asleep. When they attempted to come out, they were sliced either with knife or a cutlass and pushed back in the house to burn.

Rebels stood around the burning house and made sure no one escaped until everyone burned to death.

The next morning civilians requested the burned bodies from ECOMOG. They loaded the remains onto the back of a pickup truck and paraded to the American Embassy and other foreign diplomatic offices with tears and deep sorrow, pleading for the world to come to the aid of the Liberian people, who were tired of the brutal deaths and endless suffering. At the end of the parade, the bodies were buried in a mass grave at the Center Street Cemetery in Monrovia.

The atrocities were often misdirected, and they resulted in the torture and killings of innocent civilians. All rebel groups demonstrated the same greed, lack of discipline and depravity that characterized them. In addition to taking revenge, rebels often extorted money from the civilian population. They demanded money from families if they were prosperous and whether they worked for the government or not.

The terroristic impact of the killings was magnified by the mutilation and shameful treatment of the bodies.

One of my friends, Nicholas, was trapped at the border between Liberia and Guinea on the Liberia side when ULIMO captured Foya and surrounding villages from the NPFL. The Guineans refused to allow men to cross into Guinea from Liberia. They accepted only women and children. Nicholas, a teenager at the time, was among other men and a few NPFL rebels who were also fleeing the brutal ULIMO attack. They ran out of food completely and had to risk their lives and walk 15 to 30 miles in the bushes to abandoned villages in search of food.

The few rebels with them got so desperate and vicious that they would kill a person and eat the body parts. On one occasion, they captured a man in a village that had no food; they accused him of being in the ULIMO militia. He pleaded he was not. He said he was a Kissi from a nearby village. They asked him to speak Kissi, and even though he was speaking his ethnic language, they insisted he was not. While he was crying, one of them shot him. After he had fallen, they slaughtered him, removed his heart and other body parts, cooked them and ate them.

A few days later they went to another village in search of food. As they approached the village, my friend and others, civilians and rebels, stayed on the outskirts of the village. A rebel with an RPG entered the town alone to shoot his weapon with the intent of scaring away enemies or anyone in the community. Little did they know there was a small group of soldiers from ULIMO also watching with an RPG. The moment he stepped on the road through the village, the ULIMO militia killed him with their RPG, scattering his body into pieces. The ULIMO militia took off, and Nicholas and others went to locate his body but were only able to recover his two legs. The rebels put the two legs in a bag and placed it on Nicholas' head and took off. He was walking with the legs bleeding on him. They eventually stopped and buried the legs in a shallow grave. This propelled Nicholas and other civilians to walk back to the Makona River, and once more they negotiated with the

Guineans to allow them to cross to Guinea. The Guinea soldiers only agreed if they brought with them two five-gallon containers of red palm oil each, and they would have to swim with the oil. The women who had crossed to Guinea had left lots of oil behind. Nicholas and others swam with two gallons of oil each and crossed to Guinea.

The soldiers arrested them and accused one member of the group of being a rebel. The truth is, the rebels did not cross; all those who crossed were civilians. They tied a heavy rock on the accused's hands and feet and threw him back into the river. The Guineans then took the oil from Nicholas and others and let them travel on foot to Gueckedou.

Emmanuel, a friend of ours, and his family lived in Logan Town, Monrovia, when Price Johnson attacked and took control of part of Monrovia in 1990. One day his older brother went to find food for the family and got shot in his leg during a crossfire between the INPFL and the AFL. Even being very wounded, he managed his way home, but unfortunately, his condition became worse for the lack of treatment at home. My friend Emmanuel and family put his brother in a wheelbarrow and took the risk to take him to the hospital. On the way to the hospital, they ran into members of the INPFL. Those soldiers accused them of transporting a wounded AFL soldier, Emmanuel's mother responded saying he was not a soldier, he was her son who got shot in search of food for the family. The Leader pointed his gun at Emmanuel's brother's head and shot him dead

It broke people's hearts to learn how Liberians were killing other Liberians. There were cases when some civilians survived because of their ethnicity. A friend of ours survived when another body fell on top of him, shielding him from the soldiers' shooting.

Rice was like gold dust; money was nothing. We ate rice and beans and small clams from the river that we would boil and suck. We would also eat sugarcane. Our lifestyles changed drastically.

My school friend was walking with members of his family when they were approached by a group of Charles Taylor's rebels in trucks. They stopped to ask for "wives," so they took his 14-year-old sister and his 17-year-old cousin. He felt devastated to see them taking the young sister and cousin away. We all knew at that time what happened to women and girls who were abducted.

Besides targeting and killing groups, the rebels regularly abused their power to loot and to seek revenge during battle. There was so much hatred against one another. After they had gotten a taste for blood, rebel forces developed more interest in looting and killing regardless of ethnicity.

Because many rebels were unpaid, they were encouraged to plunder and were promised compensation in the form of loot or even a house. A child soldier put his name on a private home because he had been promised he could have every property he captured. Some other rebels destroyed properties and burned down many of them, including their contents, only to release their hatred or as a means to get revenge. They raped, tortured and arrested civilians as revenge for past grievances

Between 1991 and 1994 a group of former Doe followers and AFL officers formed a new rebel group to resist Taylor's forces. The objective of the new group was to fight against Taylor while avoiding the killing of innocent civilians. But they all committed human rights violations against civilians since the beginning of their operations. Relatives and friends told us how the troops violated people, raped girls, looted and took advantage of their power to treat people poorly. They did summary executions, tortured, arrested people under any excuse, robbed, forced children to become their soldiers, and restricted freedom of movement. When victims could not meet fighters' demands, they were often terribly punished.

Many thousands of children between nine and 14 years old were taken to join the rebel militias against their will. Charles Taylor's National Patriotic Front of Liberia (NPFL), the Independent National Patriotic Front of Liberia (INPFL), the United Liberian Movement for Democracy in Liberia (ULIMO), the Lofa Defense Force (LDF), the Liberia Peace Council (LPC) , the National Patriotic Front of Liberia-Central Revolutionary Council (NPFL-CRC), the Liberians United for Reconciliation and Democracy (LURD) and the Movement for Democracy in Liberia (MODEL) – they all had forcibly recruited children to fight, to kill, to torture and to loot for them. Even though the troops loyal to the former president, Samuel K. Doe (AFL), did not use children in their forces, they committed terrible offenses against children during the war.

All these "child soldiers" themselves suffered unnamed cruelties, as many of them were severely injured, punished, or made to watch people being tortured, cruelly murdered, and raped. Most of them were forced to take part in the killings, obliged to rape, to infringe horrible pain on people before they were killed. These children were deprived of their freedom and taken away from their families even if they didn't want to – those who resisted were killed or treated inhumanely. Others were threatened that if they didn't join their forces, the family members would be murdered in a very cruel way. These children lost their normal childhood forever.

Some kids said that they wanted to join the militia to avenge the murder of their parents or other family members, or to protect them from the warring factions. In many cases, their family had been killed. They were taught how to use AK-47s, fully automatic Kalashnikov assault rifles. Numerous "child soldiers" received cruel treatment by the same factions to which they belonged. They were beaten and forced to consume drugs to unfold their braveness. One was a blend of gunpowder with juice; other drugs were like amphetamines and cocaine

Even though crossing over into another country to harm refugees violated international law, it happened very often. The militia who belonged to the ULIMO forces passed to the Liberian refugee camp in Guinea to grab people who were trying to find a safe shelter for their lives. A woman we knew pretended to be an elderly woman to avoid their abduction. Unfortunately, not only ULIMO people did this, and they were not the only rebel group who had violated this law. Some other forces went through the border and attacked refugees in villages and towns in Côte d'Ivoire, Sierra Leone, and even as far as Ghana. The refugee camps in Côte d'Ivoire were particularly vulnerable because they were close to Liberia. Therefore, NPFL rebels easily tried to coax refugees to return to Liberia. Among the horrifying stories, there was a man who accepted and crossed over to Liberia only to find himself tied up and burned alive after the rebels dreadfully tortured him. His remains were dumped into the river.

My childhood friend Dave and I grew up together enjoying both the wellbeing of our land before the Liberian Civil War. We continued our bond through the refugee camp in Gueckedou. We sold kerosene in bottles. Most of the population in Gueckedou used kerosene to light their lamps, which provided light for the home. We would walk miles and miles around the dusty town with other kids selling kerosene. Our entire business was valued at no more than 10 US dollars.

One day my friend Dave told me he was tired and frustrated of being a refugee. He decided to go back to the village where his parents had come from in Liberia. I encouraged him to stay in Guinea. His life would be in danger in Liberia at that time. He tried to convince me that he would bring back some oil to sell and we could use the money to enhance or enlarge our kerosene business. The idea of increasing our small business sounded good, but going to Liberia was taboo for my family and me, and it also should have been for my friend and brother Dave.

But he went back to Liberia and stayed in his village, Kwesua, just when the ULIMO attacked it. My friend and other young men fled through the forest, leaving behind five elders in the community. Among them were three men and two women. They hoped that the rebels would spare their lives, given their old age. When the soldiers came into town, Dave and others were watching from their refuge in the forest. When they couldn't find the younger villagers, they grabbed the five elders, dragged them into a hut, put a chain on the door, and set it on fire. They looted as much as they could from the villagers and, making a wild scream of victory, left for the next village to continuing their massacre.

Dave and others sneaked into the village to bury the five elders. They must have joined hands until they burned to death because they found the bodies held together.

After they had buried the bodies, they went far away from the villages and deep into the woods. They could not cross the border back to Guinea because the Guineans, as usual, had closed their borders with Liberia. But the ULIMO militiamen were looking for them and went to attack Dave and the others in the bush.

Dave could not run any farther, as the rebels were very close to him. He hid behind a heap of dry dirt built by ants. His cousin Nyumah Deiyo was shot. He fell to the ground and started crying for help when he became surrounded by the rebels. One of them stood up to him and shot Nyumah Deiyo several times. Dave managed to remain camouflaged behind the hill. He maintained his breath as low as it was possible and waited until they went away. The transpiration that was covering the face was mixed with tears over the loss of his cousin.

Suddenly Dave heard someone was calling his name. He looked through the leaves and saw a group of people he knew. He didn't respond, thinking that they might have been captured by the rebels and were being used to hunt him and everybody else who could be hiding. But a familiar voice insisted, "It's me, Dave, your aunt. If you hear me, please come out. We are fine." Dave waited without saying any word. After hearing her repeat herself a few more times, he came walking from behind the hill. Helplessly and melting into tears, Dave told them what he had just witnessed. He led the group to the site were Nyumah had been killed, dug a hole in the shade and buried him.

Dave and others went back to Gueckedou, and he never returned to Liberia again until Guinea was attacked years later. Today Dave is a student at the University of Liberia. In mid-2016, after more than 15 years, he found me on social media, and we got in touch again.

Some rebels went to the extent of eating human flesh. The origins and reasons behind eating human flesh seemed to come from the Burkinabes, an ethnic group from Burkina Faso who trained Liberians to eat human flesh – when the victim was still alive. They believed that when they eat the heart of their enemy, they can acquire his or her power. They learned from the Burkina group how to extract the heart in a split second, while the victim was still alive, and eat it raw. These atrocities were not a Liberian behavior before the war.

The acts of monstrosity against human beings were often difficult to imagine as the testimony that was required before joining specific units within some militia groups.

Every group of rebels from different bands was responsible for inhuman atrocities, including rape, tortures, murder, forced recruitment, the use of child soldiers, use of drugs, abductions of bush wives, forced labor, and looting. As if all the abominable things they did to the people had not been enough, some were compelled to drink the blood of a family member and even to eat part of the body under the threat of killing a beloved one if they refused to do it.

Many Liberians who became "soldiers" came from many different ethnic groups and various sectors of society. Some were educated, but many others were less privileged and illiterate. Some received a Soviet-era PKM machine gun, and they were told that they would be executed if they tried to escape.

The unprepared militia consisted of small children to middle-aged adults. They had no formal training, and many of them were under the effects of very harmful drugs to create high dependency and which contributed to the development of severe aggressive behaviors without any regret.

There were many reasons to join the militia – among those were the promise of getting the land of families that had been killed, power, money, hatred and revenge toward those who were cruelly tortured, raped and slaughtered without any human compassion. For many of the soldiers, the consumption of drugs became their essential food and the only way to encourage them to overcome the fear of being in "combat."

Some children were abducted by the murderers of their parents. Without a family to support them, they had to choose between life or death. This lack of family members or friends led children to be involved with the militia to receive "protection" – but many of them received abuse and irreversible traumatic experiences while being forced to commit the horrendous human violations against other forces and civilians of all ages.

Children who would not be able to use a weapon were excluded and recruited for all kind of domestic abuse or sexual services. It is estimated that the use of "child soldiers" totaled over 30,000. Today, many of those children who survived are still suffering severe degrees of post-traumatic stress disorder, sometimes manifested in depression, aggression, attempts of suicide, and drug-fueled delusions.

The chaos and violence drove Liberians to seek refuge wherever they could receive any humanitarian help. A massive number of people fled. Males and females were abducted, as they were taken away to become bush wives, laborers, or combatants. Thousands of families became separated and displaced as civilians were taken away or fled. Several Krahn and another ethnicities in danger hid from the rebels in areas without proper facilities. People developed diarrhea and very severe diseases because of the bad sanitary conditions, and the water was heavily contaminated. As the food was also scarce, people were forced to venture out to buy food at the rebel lines. Not many survived in those attempts.

The deprivation of food and water was a deliberate way to kill people and instill terror. Some combatants contaminated water by throwing bodies into wells and streams. As a result of deracination and shortage of food and water, thousands of people died from malnutrition and sickness.

They usually would raid a village to get what they wanted, and if the people were unable to provide what the forces demanded, they received harsh consequences. Looting, harming people and extortions manifested the lack of discipline that characterized the rebels. They didn't even restrict themselves to necessities. They wanted everything they could Put their hands on. Many possessions were stolen. Many crops were burned.

We all needed to obtain a pass from G-2, Taylor's intelligence and administrative center, to travel along NPFL territory. It became very dangerous for men and women to move. A man would be dragged into combat or risk being killed. A woman would be raped and murdered if she dared to go alone or with children to find food or water.

The checkpoints provided combatants a means to target, extort, abuse and terrorize individuals. They demanded clothes, food, money or any other property at the crossing border or checkpoints as a "ticket" to pass without receiving any harm. At some of these places were a wall bathed in blood as a way of terrorizing people.

But passing alive and safe through the checkpoint was not a guarantee of being out of risk while moving through the countryside. Although civilians were sometimes caught in a random crossfire between the factions, they were often deliberate targets, either because of their ethnicity or being perceived as those who supported an enemy faction or the government.

Meanwhile, the Doe government attacked residents of Nimba County, especially the Mano and Gio ethnicity, because they supported the rebels. Taylor's militia targeted Doe supporters, many of whom were Krahn and Mandingo tribes, even if none of these ethnic groups had ever taken part in the war. The NPFL forces persecuted those who had been or were present employees of Doe's administration or Tolbert's administration.

But the Mandingo, Krahn, Gio, and Mano were not the only tribes who became the victims of ethnically motivated atrocities. There had also been abuses against civilians because they were Kru, Sarpo, Lorma, or Bassa during the first and second civil wars.

Virtually no one was safe. The danger of being perceived as an enemy of any combatant was very high. Sometimes the militia justified an attribution of a group affiliation to their victims as an excuse to kill them.

Rebels targeted civilians at checkpoints because they had marks that appeared to be boot marks. These marks were enough evidence to accuse the person of being a soldier and kill him. Even the appearance of being healthy or wealthy could cause rebels to pull a person out of a checkpoint line and kill him on the assumption that he belonged to the enemy forces.

Checkpoints were places to pull people out of line. The rebels forced civilians to speak their tribal languages to prove they were not Krahn or Mandingo. Those identified as belonging to those ethnicities were pulled out of the line and killed. Even there the killings were sometimes preceded by multiple forms of violence.

One of their preferable tortures was the "tabay," where the person was tied with his hands behind his back so tightly that the chest protruded, sometimes breaking the chest cavity. Tabay was occasionally followed by stabbing the victim's chest with a bayonet and causing it to explode.

In July 1990, the war between Charles Taylor's NPFL and Doe's AFL was soon increased by another fighting faction. A split developed between Taylor and a group of NPFL fighters led by Prince Johnson, who launched his group, called the INPFL, and gained control of areas in Monrovia. This new group of rebels increased the risks to civilians, as they not only became subject to violations by fighters in INFPL territory but also could be suspected of affiliation with yet another faction. Soon, Prince Johnson demonstrated his capacity to do atrocious acts against the targeted people as well as random victims. He became famous for murdering those who opposed or criticized his actions.

Indiscriminately, combatants from all factions demanded food, money, or other goods. They confiscated food and clothes from people. When victims could not meet fighters' demands, they were atrociously punished. The atrocities they performed resulted in massive numbers of internally displaced people and refugees, with dreadful torments by almost all Liberians who stayed in the country. The war provoked countless victims of other egregious human rights abuses. The first Liberian civil war was both violent and tragic. It was one of Africa's bloodiest civil wars ever.

The destruction of Liberia's innocent lives damaged Liberia so deeply that I wish I could scratch out that part from my country's history as well as from my memories.

Chapter Eight

FROM FARMERS TO REFUGEES

Man is a creature that can get accustomed to anything, and I think that is the best definition of him.

— Fyodor Dostoyesvsky,
The House of the Dead

AFTER HAVING LIVED hidden from the rebels for weeks, we were able to find a way to return to the border with our mother to cross along the Makona River in small canoes toward Guinea. Just the trip to the border was very dangerous. We had to spend several scary and dangerous hours walking just to get to the border at Solomba.

To cross the Makona River, we, as Liberians, were routinely approached by a unit of Guinean soldiers who would interview us and charge a fee for each person before we were released to proceed to the nearest village, refugee camp, or town. As soon as we crossed the border, the Guinean soldiers refused to allow my elder brother, Saah, or me to be admitted in their country because we were boys. They used to associate Liberian boys with rebels. They were stationed in a little hut just across the river on the Guinean side – about a 30-minute walk from the first Guinean village.

My mom had to meet with them in their hut and spent several minutes crying and trying to convince the Guineans not to send my brother and me across the river back to Liberia. They eventually took every penny that she had before finally letting us enter the country.

Those were dreadful times and we were so vulnerable. Children, adults, men, or women – nobody was safe. My mother knew that if we were forced to return to our country, we would be captured by the rebels and either be killed or forced to join their army as child soldiers. At the time I didn't understand the magnitude of the potential for tragedy, but I do remember how much fear we felt. My chest was blocked. I could hardly catch my breath. My brother was shaking and almost peed his pants.

Our mother came running back with her eyes red from inconsolable tears. She was still in shock from the possibility of losing us. She bent her knees and embraced us warmly when those at the checkpoint shouted for us to leave. We walked for about 30 minutes to the first village, called Kaphadou. There, we followed a man who was traveling to Gueckedou, where many Liberians who had fled the country earlier in 1990 were staying. Just before entering Gueckedou there was a river. Before crossing the bridge there was another checkpoint with Guinean soldiers who often arrested people, especially men, coming from Liberia and entering Gueckedou on charges of being rebels among others. These checkpoints were famous for their cruel behavior toward Liberians.

Since Liberian refugees were often singled out by the luggage they carried on their head while walking in a group, we were advised by a Guinean man from the village of Kaphadou to walk behind one another, leaving a few feet between us, not in a group. By doing that, we appeared to be locals who were coming from the nearby village.

We followed his advice, and as we approached the village we walked in a straight line behind one another, leaving a few feet between us. We pretended we didn't know each other; because we had very few things to carry, we looked like locals. That's how we crossed the bridge without being stopped and interrogated by the soldiers. Our mother was behind us, and I knew she was praying. After we finally crossed the bridge, we walked a long way ahead before we came together as a family. I felt that threatening eyes were spying on us through the bushes. I was so little to hold such a big fear in my soul.

Guinea is divided into eight regions: Conakry, Nzerekore, Kankan, Kindia, Boke, Labe, Faranah, and Mamou. The nation's capital, Conakry, was a particular zone. The seven other regions were subdivided into 33 prefectures. Gueckedou was a prefecture in the Nzerekore region. Even though French was their national language, Kissi and Maninka were widely spoken in Gueckedou. Therefore, we felt at home.

In Gueckedou, we were able to get registered with the UNHCR, which supplied us periodically with food and non-food items such as cooking utensils, blankets, and mats. Those first few days we stayed with a relative of my mother in the part of Gueckedou called Halimakono.

My mom found a minuscule place for us to take shelter on the outskirts of Gueckedou, in a place called Kangor. Even though the house had two bedrooms and a living room, we could only afford one room to stay in. We all lived in that bedroom: Jestina, Saah, Fayia, Fallah, my niece Sia, my mom, and me.

At this time my dad, Onike and her son Puchew, and Rose and her son Ivan had crossed to Guinea no more than three days after we left them in Voinjama. But we didn't have the opportunity to reunite yet. We did not see them for months. They crossed into Guinea from the Voinjama district side. They ate the bush yam, slept in a house built of mud, and drank the same water as the animals from the village.

The walls of houses were constructed from sticks planted vertically in the ground and tied with rope from the forest, or affixed horizontally to the vertically planted sticks and dawbed with mud. The roof was covered with zinc. Some were made of palm branches attached to sticks. Adamant ropes were used to keep the branches tied to the sticks.

Activity day at Nyeadou Refugee Camp, Guinea

There was no running water, so they had to go down to the creek to take showers – the same creek that they drank from. It was the same creek that the animals would drink water from and bathe in. They had to go further up the creek to collect drinking water. But that's the thing– as you went farther and farther up, there were other villages with people taking their baths, and there were animals in those communities too. That was ghastly.

For food they had to dig two feet down to get bush yams that were not planted by anybody – they grew in the woods by themselves, usually on the coffee farms that were owned by the Guineans. The Guineans were pretty upset and ended up charging the refugees for destroying their coffee trees because they were there in the bushes among the coffee trees, digging for bush yams. Despite the fact that we had fled our homes – leaving all that we had behind and taking almost nothing with us – we had to pay for food for weeks, some-times months, while in these places.

The unsanitary conditions in the camps and villages were repugnant. There was no protection against the dangerous bites of mosquitoes possibly transmitting malaria or other life-threatening diseases.

Weeks later, my dad, sisters and nephews had to leave the village and move to a Tekoulo town about three hours' walking distance away from where they were. Tekoulo was better than the village closer to the border, but it was still lacking in health facilities, proper sources of income, and schools.

Teta, one of my sisters, was still in Foya. When ULIMO attacked Foya, Teta crossed the border to Guekedou. She joined us in Kangor. Two months later we moved to a two-bed-room house in the same area of Kangor. This is where my dad and my sisters Onike and Rose with their sons Puchew and Ivan joined us. This house was more spacious but the roof leaked when it rained.

During the rainy season the place was cold. We didn't have enough blankets to keep us warm. There was water dripping from the ceiling in a room full of people. It was horrible. All the girls slept in one room to the left and all the boys slept in the living room at night. My parents and the little ones slept in another room. We spread mats on the floor and used blankets to soften the hard concrete floor. There were lots of mosquitoes and it was hot.

As time went on we began to settle in Gueckedou; realizing our hopes of returning home were far off at that point, we started finding more stable ways to survive. Our mother volunteered with the refugee counseling office, which provided emergency food, essential items, and services to Liberian and Sierra Leonean refugees. My sisters Rose and Teta sold roasted fish outside the N'zerekore and Macenta Parking stations, where commercial cars would line up to load passengers traveling to other places.

Refugees playing Musical Chair. Activity Day, organized by Enfants Réfugiés du Monde (ERM). Nyeadou Refugee Camp, Guinea

As time went by, my mother made soap, and my brother Saah and I would go around the neighborhood and marketplace selling it. This is how we started our lives in Gueckedou before we were able to register as refugees with the UNHCR and begin receiving food and non-food Items in Gueckedou. The food included mostly rice, cooking oil, beans and corn meal. Non-food items were cooking pots, blankets, and mats.

Months later, my sister Rose started working as a maid for an American lady named Linda, a lady who used to work for Plan Guinea. When Linda was relocated to Dakar, Senegal, she asked Rose and her son Ivan to go with her. She loved my sister so much and appreciated that Rose was a dedicated and hardworking person, respectful and committed. From Senegal, Rose made her way to the States with her son Ivan. At that time, the rest of the family lived in a three-bedroom house in Kwame, one of the many quarters in Gueckedou.

While my mother volunteered with the Refugee Counseling Office, my father taught at the G-TECH Training Center, a place established for training refugees in carpentry, auto mechanics, plumbing, electricity, and construction. As for all of us, we attended the school set up by the IRC (International Rescue Committee). Later, Teta found a job with an American NGO and was trained and worked as a social worker.

But when it seemed that we began to adapt to a new way of living, it came the time when we reached one of the saddest moments in the life of our family. After all that had happened, all of the love and sacrifices my parents had made to keep their children safe from any physical or emotional harm, there was something they couldn't prevent from happening during our time as refugees in Guinea.

My mother went to see a herbalist with an excellent reputation surrounding the curing of epilepsy to treat our youngest sibling, Fallah, who at that time was still sick. He had suffered from terrible seizures for several years. We had tried everything to relieve him from his traumatic illness and mental exhaustion.

The treatment lasted for several days in a village located in neighboring Sierra Leone. It was then when my mother and brother needed to replenish their essential supplies to eat and to sanitize themselves. Because Fallah was undergoing treatment, my mom went back home to Gueckedou, Guinea, to get some necessities. It took her almost two days to travel and return home from that village in Sierra Leone where my brother had to stay to Gueckedou, Guinea.

Just when my mother was ready to return to the village, a man from there came to our home in Gueckedou and told my parents that our brother had died. We were told two different stories about the cause of his death. One said that he had a seizure attack and died; the other was that he was shot by a Sierra Leonian rebel who, after the shootings, had claimed that he had mistakenly shot and killed my brother.

Due to the lack of a hospital, his body was brought across the border from Sierra Leone to a bordering town on the Guinea side called Nuagoa. In the process of transporting the body to Gueckedou, the rebels stopped the villagers and ordered them to bury the body right then and there. After hours of explanation and appeals by the crying villagers to the rebels, they allowed the villagers to continue with the body to Guinea. My mom and dad were on the most painful journey in their lives to the village in Sierra Leone when they met the villagers with the remains of our precious and energetic Fallah at the border town of Nuagoa. Since the body was decaying, my parents decided he would be buried there in Nuagoa. Only my mom and dad attended his funeral. We were unable to be there with him. This is the most painful thing we have experienced since then.

I never forgot to pray for Fallah every night before I went to sleep – something I believed all my siblings did. I just knew God was going to heal him. I was always afraid that if I did not remind God to take care of him, he would slip away. Sometimes I was so tired that I fell to sleep without praying. The next day, I would do a makeup prayer. This was something I never told or discussed with anybody. I believed in my soul and body that it was my responsibility to protect him and to protect him through prayers. I never knew how to react to his absence for years. I still talk to him and look up to him for guidance.

After our beloved Fallah had passed, we found that our lives had been immersed in a kind sadness that would cast away every danger, threat, and misery that surrounded our life as refugees. Nothing else mattered. It was tough to focus again on our daily duties.

As time went by we all learned from our parents to be strong and keep fighting against the most difficult challenges. I didn't see them crying, but I did see their hidden tears and suffering filtering through the tenderness of my mother's smiles and my father's eyes. Sometimes he kept his eyes far away as if he were waiting for Fallah to return home.

All of that horror surrounding our lives as refugees meant nothing compared to the loss of Fallah. We missed him terribly, and still do today. Given its sensitivity, we mourned his loss every day, but did not have conversations about it. He was the youngest of my siblings, and we missed him every day.

Most refugees in Guinea were hosted in the camps or other refugee sites while others resided in urban areas such as Conakry, originating mainly from Chad, the Democratic Republic of the Congo, Liberia and Sierra Leone. Guinea endured recurrent cross-border attacks linked to the conflicts in Liberia and Sierra Leone.

The border region – which had been home to most of the Liberian and Sierra Leonean refugees since the early 1990s – was the scene of increased combat, shelling, and military checkpoints. Former Liberian rebels were then living in Guinea as refugees. They were routinely arrested and taken away from family and friends to prisons and unknown destinations by Guinean authorities.

Resentment towards Liberian and Sierra Leonean refugees mounted, often violently, with the perception that we were responsible for security problems in Guinea. In Massadou, for example, during an armed attack which also killed 70 local inhabitants, several camps were burned down and 16,000 refugees fled on foot to Faranah, further north of Guinea. Many refugees were detained, and women were sexually abused.

The freedom of movement of refugees was severely shortened during these periods: In refugee camps like Forecariah, refugees were not allowed to leave their camps and later were only allowed to go from the camps to their fields. Also, the local authorities demanded that all refugees that were living in towns had to be relocated to camps. As a result, many refugees felt that there was no other option but to flee to their embassies in Conakry, and some like us hoped to move away to other countries.

Many fled into the forest, while others made their own way to Sierra Leone or Liberia. These were dangerous times and dangerous journeys, during which we had no security, protection, access to food assistance or health services for several months.

Unfortunately, terrible new circumstances forced us to leave Guinea and move to the Buduburam Refugee Camp near Accra, Ghana, due to the rebel attack on the Guinean Government. With almost 40,000 people, primarily Liberian refugees, it was the biggest camp in Ghana. Many refugees, like us, had fled with nothing else but courage. The purpose of fighting to keep ourselves alive produced miracles, and we kept moving safely in spite of the odds. These were very tragic days and weeks for Liberians in the Guinea Forest Region. As usual, Liberians were accused of the attack and were equally persecuted by the Guinean soldiers.

There were countless checkpoints on the roads with Guinean soldiers, who took money from us at each stop. We traveled by way of the road in commercial vehicles from Gueckedou to N'zerekore in Guinea, from N'zerekore across the Guinean border to the Ivory Coast, from the Ivory Coast to the Buduburam Camp near Accra, Ghana. The terrifying way toward Ghana lasted about three days, and the whole way we were in fear for our lives.

We had gone through hell in Guinea during our earlier years there. We had fought hard and just when we had gained a little comfort, we were forced to flee into Buduburam, Ghana, and go right back to where we had started years before when we had first arrived in Guinea. Life in Ghana was frightening. Unlike Guinea, in Ghana, we did not get any assistance from the UNHCR. We depended solely on financial support we received from my sister Rose and Husband Swaray, who were able to move a while ago to Illinois, in the United States from Senegal, West Africa.

Thanks to their contributions, my parents were able to build a three-bedrooms house in the camp. Mom once again made roasted fish, doughnuts and fried plantains for sale on the main street that passed through the center of the camp.

The camp was a place of violence and crime. Even though some refugees witnessed violent behaviors from local Ghanaians, such as rape, defilement, brutality, and stabbing of refugees every time they could, the voices of the victims were unheard. They didn't have the "right" to denounce and complain about the abuses they consistently received from local Ghanaians.

The Buduburam Camp was very unstable and sometimes dangerous. Nobody could report cases of rape or murder. Even though there was a level of uncomfortable situations at the camp, no case of murder or rape had been reported – but some atrocities had happened.

A very close friend I used to know from Liberia, called Moris, lived there with family members. He left his wife and daughter in Monrovia and came to seek travel opportunities to the United States. He had no job or source of income except what he received for water and food from a relative in America. He had been diagnosed with tuberculosis, which caused him to travel to Accra, Ghana, to get a daily treatment for two weeks. The lack of money led to inadequate medical attention. He died when he least expected it. Someone like me, who did not know about his pre-existing condition, thought that his death was very sudden. Moris was either afraid of isolation if people knew that he had tuberculosis, or he didn't know how severe his condition was. My cousin Naomi and I were on our way to visit Moris at the hospital in Accra when we heard he just died. Naomi died shortly in Liberia after I came to the States.

Ghanaians are very proud of making other Africans, and the rest of the world, believe that "Akwaaba" means "welcome." This belief is constantly experienced when someone stays in Ghana. Many Liberians support this idea. In 1996 during the notorious April 6 War in Monrovia, Liberia (the shortest but fiercest war, when Liberians were stranded onboard the Bulk Challenge Ship), other West African countries refused to allow the ship to land on their soil. The suffering Liberians who had to flee were out of food and other necessary supplies. But Ghana received them. There are numerous stories from Liberians on how the Ghanaians assisted their West African brothers and sisters.

In 2002 I witnessed a serious tension between refugees at the Ghanian police station at the entry to the refugee camp. A Ghanian had been captured by refugees during the night. For several weeks some Ghanaians went around the camp at night with long pointed irons stabbing refugees while they slept with their windows open to allow the breeze of the evening to cool their hot huts. The Liberians turned the captured Ghanian over to the Ghanian police. The police authority refused to prosecute the Ghanian and released him without any explanation. The refugees were very frustrated, and in advocacy for our rights, a huge number of refugees stayed at the police station on the camp and refused to leave until the police authority took legal action against the man who had been captured. The Ghanaians called for backup. A group of well-armed soldiers arrived at the camp and started shooting directly at the refugees and wounded many. The Ghanian radio station. Joy FM, briefly reported on the issue before it disappeared from the air completely. Joy FM said that the police had overreacted to the situation.

What we experienced at Buduburam was an example of the difficulties that the international community had in protecting and supporting refugees in prolonged refugee situations. The resulting conditions led to systemic violations of human rights of refugees under international law.

Even as refugees, we had to buy everything, including water. We bought water by the gallon. Both refugees and Ghanaians built reservoirs all over the camps and sold water from them. The water they sold from the reservoirs was brought by trucks that bought and sold water in the camp from the nearby towns. We would take a bath with as little as one gallon of water, sometimes two or three, based on what we could afford at the time. Even the pigs that my dad had raised in Liberia before the civil war had had a lot more water at their disposal than we did in Ghana. Before, we would use buckets of water on the pigs when we cleaned the pigpen, while we had to be very careful about using only one gallon of water in the Buduburam camp.

There were no jobs for the refugees. Some who received money from relatives and friends overseas invested what they got and opened phone booths. They charged by the minute to their customers who would come to the phone booths to receive and make calls overseas, mostly to relatives in the United States. Some opened shops where they sold cooked food, which not many refugees could afford to buy.

There was an indigent latrine on the camp. Most of the population went to the nearby savanna bush to defecate. As a result, people were seen by one another at a distance as they squatted to defecate. This was very unbearable, humiliating, frustrating, and unhealthy. It was very difficult and depressing to imagine that we could not even afford the very basic necessities of life and also to think about the livelihood that the rebels had taken from us.

Many people turned to their Christian faith and trusted God for His provision, good health, and a way out of the camp to the Western countries that were accepting Liberians as refugees. As a result, the refugees built many churches and places of worship in the field. It was there where I met Patience George. She was a teenager when she and her two younger siblings were separated from their parents in Liberia. They followed a group of people to the Ivory Coast in 1990. Sadly, Patience's two younger sisters went missing. As a teenager she traveled to Nigeria, Togo, Benin, and finally to the Buduburam refugee camp in Ghana in search of her sisters. There she met a Liberian lady at the Liberian Welfare Council's office in the camp.

I remember how beautiful, intelligent, and easy-going Patience was. The lady noticed several virtues in Patience and asked to be her friend. This lady, who also volunteered at the welfare office, invited Patience to come with her to her house in the camp after work. Patience honored the invitation and went with her. Upon entering the home, Patience experienced an unexpected encounter. She said that God had heard her prayers and performed a miracle. Her two sisters for whom she had been searching for a long time were there in the lady's house, and she had no idea that those two girls living with her were Patience's sisters! Patience broke down in tears of joy and thanked God for the miracle. From that day, Patience joined her two sisters in the lady's house. They lived there until the lady resettled to the United States in 2001.

Patience and her sisters stayed in the camp. In 2004 her sisters who were then teenagers, moved back to Liberia to stay with their relatives. Patience remained in the camp and studied nursing at a vocational school. Upon completion she intended to return to Liberia and find a job that would help her resettle easily. Unfortunately, she got severely sick and died. The story of Patience is one that many Liberians experienced during and after the civil war.

My parents never lost faith. Even though they had to go through very challenging experiences, they sustained in their children a high flame of purpose in life . It guided us through so many dark moments with its powerful light. From fear we learned how to fuel our courage for never giving up no matter how extreme life conditions might become. In moments of deep emotional pain and psychological disturbance, I chose to take refuge in the memories of my happy moments. I called them my rescue moments.

My parents, siblings, my friends, and I were full of life, even plagued with poverty and misery everywhere. Our parents encouraged us to be strong and resilient. I still remember how much I had longed to have wings. I used to sit on the same rock every evening to see the sun sinking in a bright orange before becoming dark, and I began to wonder about the same bright orange that insisted in announcing that a new day is born. A sudden idea of a rebirthing life after death instilled hope inside the depth of those gloomy days. What if dark is not evil but only God resting His eyes, as I do with mine when I go to sleep? What if this nightmare is another form of dreaming? What if I could choose to dream that one day I could unfold a life full of achievements and purpose in a land where we are all treated as humans with the honor and respect that life requests for itself?

My mother would call us to have dinner. I ran toward that place that became blessed by my parent's love and faith. We would pray before the meal. We ate with gratitude, knowing that many others around us in the camp wouldn't have this opportunity. After dinner, we went to sleep. I wanted to dream about life beyond the boundaries of danger and privation.

Chapter Nine

AMERICANS LIKE TO SMILE

It always seems impossible until is done.
—Nelson Mandela, 1918-2013

WHEN THE CIVIL war began in Liberia in 1989, human rights cases of abuse became rampant. Countless Liberians, like ourselves, had witnessed their families and friends being killed or tortured. More than half of the Liberians who fled the country sought refuge in Buduburam, Ghana. Many of them became too traumatized by the war to return to Liberia. People at the camp experienced the life of indigents. We all faced too many changes. It was not safe to go back to Liberia and not much safer to remain at the refugee camp in Ghana. We were some of the many refugees who had lost everything back home. Even though this situation was unbearable, we felt blessed to be alive and have the luxury of still being together as a family.

The refugee camp in Buduburam, Ghana, where we fled to after escaping a secure death from Gueckedou, Guinea, was established in 1990 to accommodate the influx of Liberian refugees who had also run away from the brutal and bloody war in Liberia. We were among the Liberian refugees who lived in the most impoverished and unhealthy conditions. While we were enduring all kinds of privation without the possibility of returning to Liberia ever again, we were hoping to receive the privilege of being relocated in a country where human rights and the opportunity to keep on evolving in our life could still be possible.

There was no life in the camp, only a way to exist. We learned to manage the psychological pressure to keep us surviving in the land of hell. The "existence" in the refugee camp was tough, especially for single parents who had lost their spouses during the civil war in Liberia.

Everything became worse when most of the refugees did not have the opportunity to work and generate money for essential needs. Some families – and thank God it was not the case for us – couldn't afford their children's daily meals, which in many cases pushed kids into immoral activities to survive. It was sorrowful to see innocent children trying to subsist on the streets by themselves. Unfortunately, some of them became victims of sexual abuse and rape by unscrupulous adults, which led many of these kids to unwanted pregnancies.

The scarcity of water and proper sanitary conditions were some of the problems we had to deal with. Water was sold from commercially operated mobile tankers as well as in plastic sachets, while many refugees depended on rainfall or water from wells to survive. We had to pay for the water we drank and even to use a toilet. There was no functional pump for the refugees in the settlement, leaving a considerable number of refugees without safe drinking water. Therefore, we were all exposed to severe diseases, some deadly due to a lack of sufficient health care.

We didn't have all the things we were accustomed to having at home before the Liberian Civil War. Essential things had disappeared, and among those was education. Most children in the refugee camp didn't have the opportunity to attend schools due to hardship and the inability of their parents to provide a formal education for them. This situation made it challenging for refugees who couldn't afford to send their children to Ghanaian schools.

Eventually, many kids began living on their own. Some who had served as breadwinners for their families were vulnerable to exploitation and varying types of abuses, including child labor, prostitution, and crimes. Wayward children as young as 13 years old were seen pushing wheelbarrows while others, especially girls, went around to wash clothes for a living.

I knew that my parents had built the bonds of an unbreakable family under the distress of the most terrible challenges. Their hope and courage were admirable. I still wondered at moments of great despair what was keeping us alive, inside and out. Perhaps our "evergreen land," the yard where we used to live, was still developing trees, flowers, crops, and hopes somewhere within us? What was the force of our fortitude made of? Our Kissi blood? Granddad's charms that he used to hold for his luck and ours? Was it God and the faith in His divine compassion that had rescued us from horrifying death? Or had it been the combination of everything?

Despite the discouraging situations we experienced every day, my parents never lost their faith that something might appear to rescue us from our misfortune. My mother's tenderness and my father's fortitude prevented us from becoming physically sick while helping our minds to remain healthy and resilient, even while facing the most psychologically strenuous pressures.

If life had not punished us enough at the refugee camp, my dad got a brain tumor. Considering the circumstances in the camp, he didn't have the opportunity to receive proper treatment. As a result of the inadequate assistance he received, my father began to gradually lose the sight from his bad eye, and then the other, until he became irremediably blind.

Everything seemed to get darker until one day, a promising light coming from faraway shores began to open to those possibilities we had dreamed of achieving. My sister Rose, along with her husband, Joseph Swaray, made available the opportunity for us to be resettled with her in the United States. Once we heard the news, I began to jump, run, and dance. How much we had longed for a rebirth in the land where we could be treated as human beings! Respect, honor, achievements, progress, evolution, even glory, why not? It was just a matter of dreaming with all our hearts to see things happening – that was what I had always heard about America.

Every step, every year, moved us forward toward the promising land of opportunities. It took five years to overcome all the processes, and the last part was learning about America, its culture, its past, and how everything began there until the

United States developed such an amazing country. I immersed myself into studying about America with so much passion that I could have become a professor of American history. I walked through the dirty streets of our refugee camp in Ghana, but I didn't see anything miserable surrounding my life – my heart was so much ahead and beyond. My mind was walking miles and miles, thousands of miles ahead. I was anticipating our life in Illinois with such unbeatable faith.

And it came the blessed day when we were about to depart for the United States of America. America... we had everything ready to begin a new life as Americans until something went very wrong. The timing of our departure was about to coincide with one of the most terrible terrorist attacks ever committed in the United States. September 11, 2001, would lead the world to dramatic changes, and our travel was postponed to time indefinite. This was very frustrating and arduous. We were left in Limbo.

The excitement that our long suffering as refugees had come to an end was no more. All the big efforts Rose had made were temporarily lost. Our hope for our family to be together once again, after Rose and Ivan had left us in Guinea years ago, was denied. Most importantly, our father, who had gone blind from a brain tumor, would have to wait an indefinite time again before receiving better treatment. He also began suffering from severe headaches and hallucinations. The longer he was away from proper medical assistance, the worse his situation grew and the more depressed our entire family became.

Everything was very scary. We had waited years for this moment, and to get this close and see it slip away was very discouraging and painful. These were all things that refugees went through every day, all the time. Tomorrow is not promised. You have no control of your life. Anything could happen. We patiently and prayerfully waited with no communication from the immigration office on our departure status until we were notified in June of 2002 that we were scheduled to travel to the States. This was one of the best things – if not the best thing – that had happened to us in more than 10 years.

Those few days before we left we were experiencing mixed feelings of happiness and sadness. Our sister Onike and her two kids, who were both under the age of 10, were unable to travel with us. They were disqualified during the interview. My nephew Joseph, who was very close to my dad, became incredibly sad when he was told he could not travel with us to America.

Teta (white shirt), Hadja (red t-shirt and blue jacket). Accompanie to bus stop on Buduburam Camp, Ghana. Departure day to the U.S

A few minutes before we boarded the bus to the Kotoka Airport in Accra from the Buduburam Camp in Ghana, he knelt next to my dad, laid his head on Papa's lap, and cried as Daddy patted him while promising that he would send for him sooner than he might think, and Joseph released a cheerful smile.

It was very sad for us to leave relatives and friends in the camp. On the other hand, our dream to travel to the United States and transform our lives from the long suffering had finally begun to come true. Our relatives and friends hoped that we would be able to help them back at the camp.

The night before our trip, our church members, neighbors, and friends all gathered at our refugee home, praising God with us through songs and prayers. Some brought us African fabrics as gifts. The next day, more than 20 people accompanied us to the bus station at the camp and bid us goodbye as we drove away to the Kotoka Airport in Accra.

I will always remember that as I walked through the airport how deeply I breathed and then I boarded the KLM aircraft. It was hard to believe we were about to start our new life away from danger, away from death. An unbearable anguish had stabbed extreme fears in my heart as the pilot announced our takeoff. My panic was that something bad might happen again to prevent us from arriving at the rebirth of our lives. I just needed to be detached forever from the ground that had been irrigated by the blood of so many innocent people. Above and beyond the horror. As if it had never occurred to us or to others.

I looked back, and my mother was comfortably sitting next to my father. I saw how strongly they held their hands. The murmur of the turbines told me that we were finally safe. In the clouds, I saw myself above all the distress we had experienced in the last 11 years. No more dangerous moments would take us back to hell. It was very rewarding to see everything from a calming blue sky. Amazingly different.

We flew for about seven hours from Accra to Amsterdam, where later we would board another KLM aircraft and fly for almost nine hours from Amsterdam to Chicago. The moment had finally come. Upon our arrival at the Chicago airport, we headed toward Rose, her family, the church members, and friends who had anxiously waited for us.

The airport was very busy and huge. It was like an amusement park. I'd never seen anything like this in my whole life. I hadn't even dreamed that all these things could exist. Corridors were spreading in different directions. There was a large food court with all kinds of meals and beverages tempting everyone to try something comforting before their trips. We kept walking, and I saw a large store with everything to pamper one's desire for comfort and luxury. Gift stores. Magazines, candies, books. I just wanted to stop at any of them, but we were in a hurry to meet our new life. People were running, some walking fast, others slow. I could see how everybody was full of life. No one had any idea where we were coming from....and, for an instant, not even I.

Those terrible days were being washed away, vanished, erased by all the love and compassion we received upon our arrival. Emotions, feet, breath, heartbeats, everything, was agitated inside us, propelling our motion toward a heavenly encounter. Rose, splendid Rose, ran and gave each one of us a warm hug and ended with my dad, who was in a wheelchair. When she had left for the United States, my dad had good vision and no signs of eye problems. We had told her over the phone about his condition, but she had not seen any pictures, so she did not quite understand what it was like. She cried tears of joy and also sadness for our dad. He looked very sick and had not aged well.

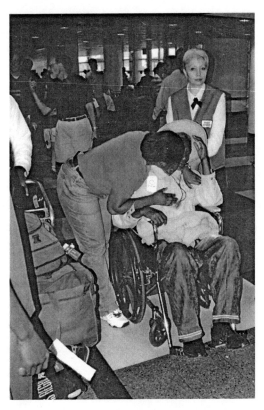

Rose Welcomes Dad. 2002 O'hare International Airport, Chicago

In my eyes and mind, she was still Rose. The beautiful, talkative, fast, and very active Rose. Ivan, the baby, who the last time we saw him in Guinea had become a big handsome and smart boy. Mr. Swaray, as usual, welcomed us with a big smile. Rick Carson and Lin Tornquist from Gary Church also welcomed us with a big smile. Yea Dunar, whom to this day we still know, also welcomed us to the States and Wheaton, Illinois, very happily.

We left the airport in Gary's church van driven by Rick; Rose talked the whole way through. She was so excited. She assured us that the long suffering was over and that everything "will be much better here." Our first stop was at the church, Gary United Methodist Church, on Main Street in Wheaton.

It was my first time in almost 11 years that I had seen so much food. At the church, we were led to Garmor Hall in the basement where there was a long table filled with all kinds of food and drinks that had been prepared for us by members of the church. We began to experience the generosity of the church family who still today remain our friends. They were always smiling, very gentle, and kind.

The church received us with a welcoming treat for all of us. After they had heard a little about our story, they sympathized with us and were equally happy that all the terrible days and suffering had come to an end. They all introduced themselves to our family. I'll never forget how careful they were in pronouncing our names and making sure that they were saying them well. It was there where we met our host families.

L-R Princess, Teta, Daddy, Rose and Hadja, 4th of July 2003, Wheaton IL.

Rose and family, Gary Church, and World Relief had planned our first two weeks in Wheaton. We were a total of 11 that just arrived from Ghana. Church members hosted some of us for the first week until we could get a space that could receive us all. My parents and niece Sia stayed with Rose and her family. Teta and her daughter Hadja stayed with Beverly Holze and family, and Jestina and her daughter Princess stayed with Dave Row and his wife Virginia; Saah and Fayia stayed with Walt and Kathy Henderson. Moses and I stayed with the Austins – Bill, Vickie, and their son Will.

Dad and Walt Henderson, 2002 at the Henderson's, Wheaton IL.

I couldn't believe it when I finally had access to pure and clean drinking water. I spent a little time looking through the water running from the tap only to be delighted with how transparent it was. I also brought my nose close to the water to find out if it had any smell, and it smelled drinkable and refreshing. There was also electricity and so much comfort in the house. I had given up any hope of spending time in an authentic humanitarian environment. I walked around very cautiously so as to not break anything in that perfect house.

Oh, my first shower in years! I still remember how happy I felt when I took that warm shower in that beautiful bathroom. I used a sponge with a liquid soap that smelled of citrus like the lemon grass leaves that my mother used to harvest in our evergreen yard. I believe I spent about 30 minutes letting the water run, caressing my entire body. I felt that it was removing not only dirt, tension, and exhaustion of a long trip, but also those dark energies from the terrible environments and pain I had experienced. I looked at myself in the mirror, and I saw my inner smile sculpting a happy gesture onto a face that had been punished by the pain of those days.

The bedroom smelled of lavender blended with vanilla. My fingers couldn't resist the idea of walking over that cozy blanket, and I pulled back the covers of the bed as if the day were opening the petals of a white fragrant flower. I fell into a profound sleep that night, and each consecutive night in that perfect bed. No more nightmares. No more fears of sudden death. It was the most comfortable experience I had had in more than a decade.

The first two weeks we were full of appointments to obtain our Social Security cards, State IDs, and medical checkups. Rose and her husband, Joe, together with World Relief and the church, made everything possible for us to get all the appointments and on time.

Just as we were told during our cultural orientation in Ghana, Americans like to smile. We could not help but notice smiling faces everywhere we went, especially at church. The streets were breathtaking – clean with beautiful trees all around. Even the air smelled different and very pleasant, and the lawns were green. Everything was just perfect– kids and their parents in a restaurant or church, seeing families picnicking in the park, going to and from the grocery store.

My beloved parents felt as if they were walking in heaven. My mom was excited that all of us, her children and grandchildren, would have the opportunity to acquire an excellent education again. We all received better health care, and we were finally released from the bad health conditions we suffered in the camps, including the despair of going through unemployment and hopelessness.

My father received excellent health care at the Central DuPage Hospital after we arrived in the area in 2002. I will never forget the name Dr. Ross, his surgeon from Central Dupage Hospital. My dad had two surgeries which removed the brain tumor that provoked his blindness. The surgery saved his life and he did not have to suffer a constant headache for a good while. I felt wonderful and hopeful when I began living in the United States.

I became a reborn human being. The first thing I wanted to do was to go to school. The World Relief Organization gave us a tour through the community college College of Dupage (COD). It was my first time seeing a campus or school so big, well-equipped, and beautiful, with thousands of students. At the time, we lived approximately five miles from the school. The only transportation I had was a bicycle that I received from my friend and host, Bill Austin.

I peddled my bike to the school now and then as if I was a student there. I sat in the library and looked up books, even though we had a community Library in Wheaton that was much, much closer to home. I would ride to COD just to get the feeling of its magnificence. At this time, I did not know that I could use the computer as a non-student until one day my friend Bill told me.

Being able to go online gave me the opportunity to communicate with friends and family back home in Africa. In Ghana, we had to pay per minute to use the internet. Therefore, with free online access I wanted to spend as much time there as possible! I continued visiting the college until a week after I got my TSSN. It was then when our family friend Beth from Gary Church gave me the opportunity of an interview for what ended up being my first job with Bernald Mcguan. She said to me: "Gus, Bernard is a member of our church and does construction work; give him a call and tell him that I gave you his number. He might have some work for you."

I was very excited but I did not know what to expect. I was ready to work and hopefully save up to buy my first car and start school at COD in the fall. But July was almost over and the fall quarter began early in September, and I wasn't sure how much I could save.

With the information from Beth. I ran to the folks greeting one another after the service and hunted Bill down for a ride. As usual, he accepted the request and dropped me at home. I picked up the phone when I got to my room, stood at the window, and gave Bernard a call. Before I was done introducing myself, he interrupted and said, "Gus! Beth told me you are a hard worker." I said, "Yes, sir, I am," and he replied, "Are you ready to work?" I said, "Yes, sir." "Can you work today?" "Yes, sir." "What's your apartment number?" "D-19, sir." "OK, come down in 45 minutes, and I will pick you up so we can do some work."

In exactly 44 minutes, I looked through the window of our living room that overlooked the parking lot. I saw a white Chevy truck with a man in the driver's seat on the phone. I opened the door, staring at the car, and the man on the phone waved at me. I flew downstairs and sat in the passenger seat of the car. He shook my hand, backed up, and drove away. He asked me if I knew Gary. I said, "Yes, I go to church there." He said, "Me too, but not the church. Gary, Indiana." I said, "No, sir." He responded that we were going to Gary to do some work that he had already started.

When two hours later we arrived at the Olympia Recreation Construction Company in Gary, Indiana, he showed me around the carpenter shop, showing me the different machines. He took me to the back and told me a brief story about the train and the train track.

It was time for business. He presented me with some metal materials covered with the thick plastic that had to be installed in a playground he was working on. He handed me some cleaning tools, gloves, and cleaning solutions, and asked me to clean as much as I could. He demonstrated the technique to me on one of the pieces and took off to another side of the property. I cleaned and cleaned everything. Hours later, he came back and said, "Good job. It's time to go home." On our way home, he looked at me and said, "Good job today, you are hardworking." This is how I began my first job in the United States.

He picked me up at five in the morning for the next few weeks. Bernard reminded me a lot of my dad – always finding something else to do. He was a very hardworking man who inspired me to work harder and harder. Even as the boss, he was the first to arrive in the morning and the last to leave. I did the same. Bernard had no ego. He did everything, from picking up trash to operating the bobcat. He dug the soil and erected poles, he used the handsaw to cut metals, and he assembled playground equipment. He made our workplace a place to teach us how to value and honor the blessing of having a job without knowing he was teaching. He told me stories of his experiences in other countries. We talked politics, religion, and family. He was a family man who loved and respected his family very much. It was very important to him to attend events with the family and be there for dinner. Bernard, like my father, was down to earth with a genuine commitment to his family, work, and church. At church, my boss is a dishwasher. On Sundays, ever since I had known him, he would wash the coffee pots and kitchen utensils and make coffee for the congregation.

Today as a contractor I can work harder and more consistently due to what Bernard inspired in me. When overseeing a project, I fully commit myself. I am also proud to say that with the help of my uncle, we assembled the first firetruck Bernard ever installed on a playground. He told me that the accuracy and time we spent to assemble the fire truck made him trust my intelligence and skills even more. Thumbs up for me.

Even though I left work with Bernard in the fall to attend the College of Dupage, I still would work for him occasionally. I enrolled at the College of DuPage in the autumn of 2002. At that time it had a quarterly system. Words cannot express how excited I was to be a student at COD. Thanks to David Brewer, who helped me in the enrollment process and introduced me to Sue Weeks in the admissions department of the college. I went there, took the test, and started school in the fall.

Everyone needs a Dave in his or her circle of friends. Dave has one of the most extraordinary personalities I have ever seen. He has a unique way of giving hope and bringing light to any dark situation with a smile, care, and solutions. Over the years, I have approached Dave with series of problems, from getting a ride to school to the death of a loved one. On every occasion, he helped me and gave me hope. To my family and friends, I called him my rock.

L – R Princess, Gus and Hadja, 2003 at Gary Church court yard, Wheaton IL.

My first day at this new school I felt I was walking in a dream. What a beautiful fall! I'd never seen an autumn palette before. Everything was dressed in warm oranges, ochre, yellows, some greens, with the wind mixing everything together.

The school exceeded my expectations. I couldn't believe my luck of having been blessed with this opportunity. As students, we had everything we needed. Countless computers and extraordinary computer labs. A well-equipped library. Multiple buildings. A gym. A basketball court. Various theaters. A large cafeteria. Very well qualified staff. Everything was beyond imagination. I couldn't avoid comparing it to the one I had attended in the refugee camp. I realized, once again, how blessed my life has always been. I was ready to get my feet wet and start running.

Every day I rode my bike with the enthusiasm of an airline pilot embracing the wind. Soon I learned to become an achiever. I successfully completed the four classes of the first semester. But something was missing in the environment of our school classes. Among the luxury of having everything available to fulfill each student's needs, there was a lack of respect for the teachers. I wasn't accustomed to this in our Liberian schools nor the schools at the refugee camps. Nevertheless, I committed myself to absorbing all the knowledge I could to improve my skills and my life.

My favorite teacher was Mr. Robert Dixon-Kolar. I called him Mr. Kolar. He was tall and very friendly. He spoke gently, clearly, and with a genuine smile on his face all the time. I used to love his sweaters. Wearing warm clothes wasn't something I grew up with. Liberia has tropical, hot, and very humid weather all year round. So, I was delighted to see the colorful and nicely designed sweaters that Mr. Kolar used to wear on the cold days.

Being much aware of this opportunity, I absorbed as much information as I could. I loved learning. I wanted to improve my life through this opportunity to become a better me. But in spite of everything I found myself behind the rest. Soon, I realized that most of my classmates were faster readers than I. Their sentence structure was also better than mine. Therefore, I visited Mr. Kolar quite a few times to catch up and improve my writing ability. Mr. Kolar taught me English 091, 092 and 101. He encouraged me to apply to the Global Studies Program, designed to provide the necessary skills to navigate the global challenges of our world. I was immediately accepted. It was here I met some of the coolest people on campus: Dominique Steward, Global Studies coordinator; Nancy Wajler, Ed.D., Career Services director; Shamili Ajgaonkar, biology professor, among others.

All the parents of the students were invited to the orientation meeting. I saw my mother gently entering the large room. We made eye contact, and I saw tears rolling down her soft cheeks, and yet she smiled. I closed my eyes for a few seconds, and our past made its presence. We were all growing up in our huge yard in Liberia – our evergreen land, later darkened by the claws of an impious civil war. The endless days of fleeing along the most dangerous path where only a Divine would have the power to keep us alive.

The sudden voice of the host took me back to the event. The head of the program, Zinta Konrad, opened the meeting by sharing the goals of the program. For the first time, I heard that we should remove the word "foreign" from our choice of words when referring to people from different geographical backgrounds. Zinta wisely said: "If we talk referring to others as "foreigners," it would build a potential distance or separate ourselves from them in a negative way." Listening to her message I found myself experiencing a rare state of security – a human who could be considered human. As someone who had been oppressed and ferociously ripped out of his roots, it brought me happiness to see myself there.

The atmosphere was so peaceful, loving, educative, respectful, and promising. And besides the nutritive emotional feeling that was feeding my spirit, they had also spread a wide variety of food all over the buffet – plenty of it. I couldn't resist comparing so much abundance to our past experiences, after having been undernourished in the fields where we lived as refugees in danger for so many years.

At the end of the program, we all took turns to say what we had heard and our thoughts about the program. When my mom's time began, she stood up gently, almost in slow motion, as someone who was emerging from the darkest years of her life. With tears of joy, she said: "I just want to thank you all for the opportunity of allowing my son to be part of this program. To see him here among you is a blessing. I just want to thank you all."

Then she broke into more tears and slowly sat down.
I couldn't help but be moved too. I knew some of the million things that might be going through my mother's mind
as she sat attentively listening to the entire program. She
might have been thinking about the many atrocious things
we'd been through. Our sufferings. The terrible loss of her
youngest son, my beloved brother Fallah. The life that had
been stolen from us. The danger we survived. And, although
it might sound too incredible to be true, we were stepping
into a promising future. A rebirth. Life had given us a second
chance, and we were there, together, to honor it and leave our
ghastly past behind.

At the end of the event, I walked to my mother. She was
standing in the crowd with elegance and pride. My sister Rose
had bought her a colorful dress that enhanced her beautiful
presence. In the middle of the room, we melted in a deep
hug. Then, slowly, we headed toward the door where our host
shook our hands and thanked us for our presence.

Outside it began to be spring. I felt it in the air and in
our hearts.

****

Two years later, I completed the program with a diploma
as a global scholar. Mr. Kolar had been very helpful during
the entire process. Even the local newspaper wrote an article
about the program, mentioning my name as one of the first
graduates of the Global Studies Program from Wheaton. My

good friend David Brewer saw the article and handed me a copy of the paper, which I still have today.

This moment became a reminder of one of my first successes in the United Sates, mainly Wheaton, Illinois. This little town, 30 miles west of Chicago, became an extended home from home. Gary Church also sits north of its Main Street. A church I am deeply attached to, not only because of its beautiful structure, cozy place of worship, well-decorated altar or colorful windows, but for the cheerful hearts that it gathers here to worship and serve its community and humanity around the world.

As often as it can be to go through the transition of pastors in the Methodist church, I am proud to say I have seen the shift of four pastors at Gary Church in the past 14 years: Pastor Rick Carlson, Pastor Ed Tevrin, Bishop Tracy Smith Malone, Pastor Jimmy and Rev. Dr. Christopher Pierson. All of these pastors, in their different styles of preaching and teaching, thought and encouraged their congregant to love, care and serve. This message and practice got me deeply attached to Gary. I can see and feel what they preach and teach. It is manifested in the tremendous work and service of Debra Hafner, Barbara and Don Garlinger, Lin Turnquist, Pastor Jonathan Crail, Mike Capra, Patsy Sorrell, Pastor Sandra Sagehorn, Teresa and Dave Exner, Tony Asta, Betsy Boyd and so many more. I have not been obligated in any way, shape or form to mention the name of any one of these honorable people. Knowing them individually, if I had asked their permission, they would insist I do not mention their names. I would rather

be shy and discreet to mention the names of those that torture and destroy humanity than those who restore hope, give
life and improve humankind.

I remember so vividly the son of my mother's best friend
who threatened to kill me and my brother. I don't want to be
shy to tell the world of a friend, career coach, speaker and TV
host named Vickie Austin who calls me her son, treats me like
one and inspired me to keep my head up and reach for the sky.

What story should I be the proudest of? The story of the
rebel that threatens to kill my mother if she continuously
insisted that he not take her daughters with him to Foya?
Or the story of a soft-spoken friend and pastor from Illinois
named Rick Carlson who was there to transport us, encourage
us and pray with us minutes before our dad would undergo a
surgery we did not quite understand?

When you have been torn apart, it is uncommon to forget
the hands that hold you. The rebels destroyed my innocence
and took away my chances of going to college; Rick not only
encouraged me to go to college, but he also bought my first
set of books to start college. He stood by my family and
me through thick and thin. His presence continues to be a
breath of fresh air. He is the encouragement behind this piece
of writing. I believed that my purpose on this earth would
be incomplete if I didn't tell the world about my encounter
with Rick and all those who helped my family and me. It's
not about us. We are just the elements of the story. The point
is to shed light on what's happening in parts of the world
where not much of this is known. On the other side of the

coin, I want that those who live in these places could continue persevering and recognizing that there is a Rick Carlson, a David Brewer, a Vickie Austin and a Bill Austin in the great United States of America. Above all, there is a God that cares. A God through whom we are blessed to have organizations like World Relief Dupage/Aurora. A Christ-centered organization with 80 plus staff members partnering with over 125 local churches and 800 volunteers to serve more than 5000 refugees and immigrants yearly.

Gus and Bill, 2016 Wheaton IL

As much as I enjoyed the computer technology program at the college with state-of-the-art networking and computer maintenance labs, the Global Studies Program provided me with the tools necessary for employment and progress in any discipline. Every seminar of the program was useful and could be applied to real life challenges.

Our world has become so versatile that in every community there are people of different ethnicities, cultures, beliefs, religions, and political affiliations living among one another. To flow with success through multicultural behaviors was one of the many tools I received from this program. Today, those learned skills have actively contributed to my career as a low-voltage contractor. There was no way I would be able to professionally navigate through different cultures without learning how to embrace diversity.

Looking back at my country and the civil war, I feel deeply sad for those who didn't have the opportunity to be rescued from the inhumane behaviors. I can say that the absence of moral values, inadequate education, extreme poverty, corruption, and intolerance to other ethnicities and cultural practices created the terrain that favored the development of countless atrocities. The wounds have not yet healed, and the pain can still be heard from afar.

The End

CPSIA information can be obtained
at www.ICGtesting.com
Printed in the USA
LVOW12s0259290318
571535LV00001B/59/P